Clara's KOOKY COMPENDIUM of THIMBLETHOUGHTS and WONDERFUZZ

Best Poetry Books Ever!

Clara's Kooky Compendium of Thimblethoughts and Wonderfuzz

Our principal reads poems from this book for morning announcements

***GREAT MORNING:* Poems for School Leaders to Read Aloud**

***HERE WE GO:* A Poetry Friday Power Book**

This book has the poem "Can You Wiggle Like a Worm?" SUPER FUN!!!

***HOP TO IT:* Poems to Get You Moving**

***PET CRAZY:* A Poetry Friday Power Book**

The Poetry Friday Anthology for Celebrations

Bilingual! Spanish + English!! Makes me feel MUY FELIZ!!

The Poetry of Science

Uncle Frank's drawings are in this big book of science poems!!!

Things We Do

Things We Eat

Things We Feel

Things We Wear

What Is a FAMILY?

What Is a FRIEND?

What Is Hope?

***YOU JUST WAIT:* A Poetry Friday Power Book**

Clara's Kooky Compendium of Thimblethoughts and Wonderfuzz

by Sylvia Vardell & Janet Wong

drawings by
Frank Ramspott

THIS WEEK IN OUR CLASS

Mon
Tue
Wed
Thu
Fri
Sat
Sun

Mrs. Booker is giving us each a notebook.
We already have writing journals.
What is this new notebook?

Mrs. Booker says:
Each of you
is going to make your own
COMPENDIUM.

WONDERFUZZ
Are humans the only animals who tell stories?

It will be full
of important facts and trivia,
questions and quotes, poems and stories,
things you find online or in books,
things you want to remember.

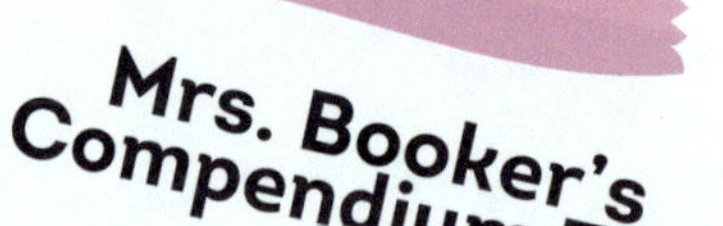

Mrs. Booker's Compendium Tips

1. Collect facts and trivia
2. Jot down questions
3. Copy or cut-and-tape poems
4. Add drawings or illustrations
5. Put in anything you want

You can print and cut and paste
or doodle —

Put in anything you want!

THIMBLETHOUGHT
Scientists say that people who doodle can remember 29% more than people who don't doodle.

I am super-excited
to be making a compendium.
I ask:
Can I glue my Uncle Frank's drawings
into my compendium?

Mrs. Booker says:
Put in ANYTHING you want.

My BFF Elise asks:
Can I put things like old ticket stubs
and list my favorite scary movies
and make it part compendium,
part junk journal?

Mrs. Booker says:
Put in ANYTHING you want.
We will work on it in class
every day this week.
You can choose to work on it
at home too.

Let's get started!

WONDERFUZZ

What is the most famous book in the world? [I looked it up: It's the Bible! 5 billion copies have been sold!]

THIMBLETHOUGHT

The best-selling children's book of all time is The Little Prince (Le Petit Prince), which has sold over 200,000,000 copies since it was published in 1943. It was written by French author Antoine de Saint-Exupéry.

Mrs. Booker is going to give us lots of writing exercises for this compendium project. Here's our first one.

EXERCISE #1: AUTHOR BIO

Put a picture or drawing of yourself in your compendium. Write your author bio and add it to your book.

WONDERFUZZ

Grownups always ask you "what do you want to be when you grow up?" but I don't know. How do I decide when so many different things are interesting to me?

Here's a drawing of me (Clara) by my Uncle Frank

THIMBLETHOUGHT

The word "autobiography" comes from the Greek roots "auto" (meaning "self"), "bio" (meaning "life"), and "graph" (meaning "write").

ABOUT THE AUTHOR

Clara is a fourth grade student at Mergeler Elementary who loves animals. She spends her free time baking cookies, eating popsicles, Zooming with her Uncle Frank who lives in Germany, having sleepovers with her best friend Elise, skateboarding, and playing soccer, pickleball, basketball, and video games. She lives with her mother, her younger brother James, her little sister Vera, Wilby (AKA Boss Dog of the Universe), and Rosie the Cat.

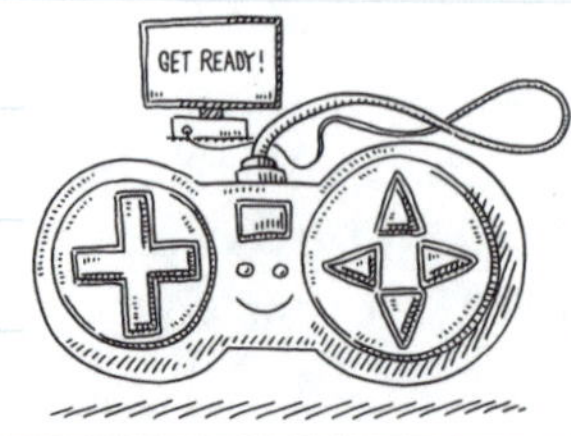

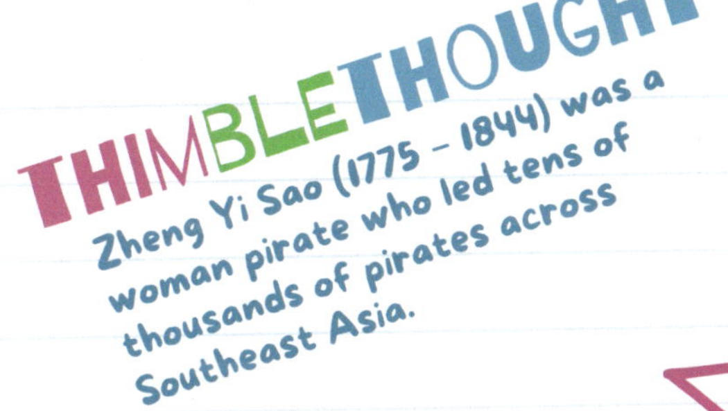

THIMBLETHOUGHT

Zheng Yi Sao (1775 – 1844) was a woman pirate who led tens of thousands of pirates across Southeast Asia.

In This Journal

by Eric Ode

A carpenter can keep the things she makes.
A baker just might keep the things he bakes.
A pirate likes to keep the gold she plunders.
But me, I am a thinker,
and I keep my thoughts and wonders.

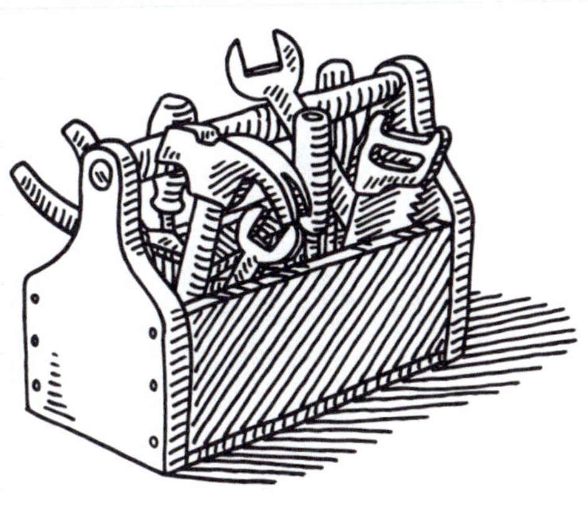

WONDERFUZZ

I wonder how people know if they want to be a baker or carpenter? I definitely don't want to be a pirate!

THIS IS MY ~~JOURNAL~~ COMPENDIUM
by Clara

In this ~~journal~~ compendium
I will write down things I know
even if they're just tiny little thoughts
the size of a fairy thimble
** THIMBLETHOUGHTS **

and I'll write down questions that pop into my head
even if they're just fuzzy wonderings

** WONDERFUZZ **
and I will also put in LOTS AND LOTS of poems
and super-neat drawings by my Uncle Frank
(who is my favorite artist).

If you're reading this
(and I know that YOU are reading this, Mrs. Booker),
that is A - O K because
this is not a private diary-journal.
It's a fact-filled, fun
COMPENDIUM!

THIMBLETHOUGHT

Some people think that the ancient Egyptians created the question mark in the shape of a cat's tail because they loved cats!

WONDERFUZZ

When we write, do our words become brain tattoos?

Clara's 10 Favorite Fuzzy Things

1. puppies
2. cotton candy
3. bumblebees (to watch, not to touch!)
4. my fuzzy socks
5. our fake sheepskin blanket
6. my fuzzy bear
7. kiwi fruit
8. baby chicks
9. kittens
10. my WONDERFUZZ ideas!

compendium (com·pen·di·um)
pronunciation: come-PEN-dee-um
part of speech: noun
definition: a large collection of information in a book

com = together
pendere = weigh (or hang) on a scale

so . . .
a compendium weighs stuff together?

THIMBLETHOUGHT

Most countries have compendiums or compilations of law used by judges; for example, the 613 commandments, or the United States Code.

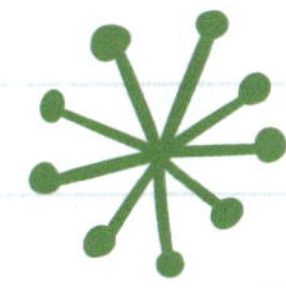

A compendium is
a collection,
a roundup of facts.

It's a handbook,
a summary,
a digest — it's packed

with trivia or numbers
or all
of the above . . .

And mine
will be stuffed with
poems I love!

WONDERFUZZ

Is there a compendium of laws of the universe?

EXERCISE #2: POET LIST
Keep a list of names of poets whose poems you like. Look for poems by them to print and tape into YOUR compendium.

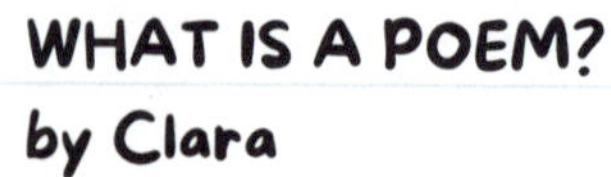

WHAT IS A POEM?
by Clara

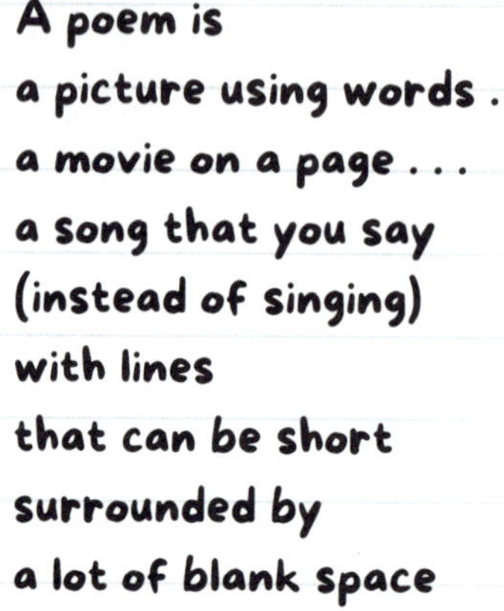

A poem is
a picture using words . . .
a movie on a page . . .
a song that you say
(instead of singing)
with lines
that can be short
surrounded by
a lot of blank space

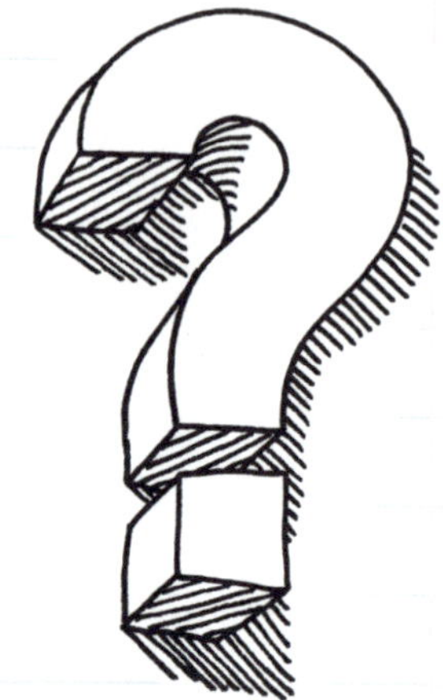

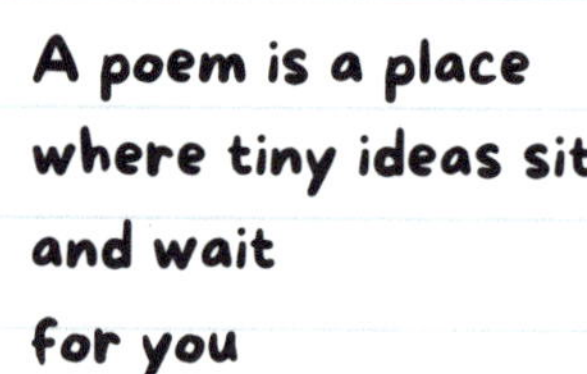

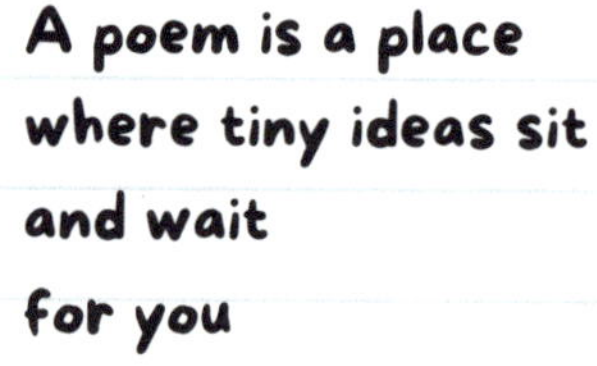

A poem is a place
where tiny ideas sit
and wait
for you

THIMBLETHOUGHT

The word "anthology" comes from the ancient Greek words "anthos" meaning "flower" and "-logia" meaning "collection." It originally meant a collection of flowers, but now means a collection of poetry, literature, art, or music.

An ANTHOLOGY is a book with poems
by lots of different people.
My compendium will be an anthology
with lots of facts added to it.
How will I find poems for my compendium?
Mrs. Booker brought in a big pile of poetry books
and gave us a list with names of popular poets.
We will look for their poems this week
and will write them down
or print them out and cut-and-tape.
Scissors up, Buttercup: it's poem-hunting time!

List of Poets

Alma Flor Ada
Verrena Diane Anderson
Dolores Andral
Marcie Flinchum Atkins
Kevan Atteberry
Lisa Billa
Robyn Hood Black
Merry Bradshaw
Jay Brazeau
Sandy Brehl
Calef Brown
F. Isabel Campoy
Yangsook Choi
Cynthia Cotten
Mary E. Cronin
Hollie Dagata
Leslie Degnan
Kristy Dempsey
Joanne Emery
Margarita Engle
Janet Clare Fagal
Douglas Florian
Patricia J. Franz
Marilyn Garcia
Van G. Garrett
Charles Ghigna
Avis Harley
David L. Harrison
Jane Heitman Healy
Sara Holbrook
Lyn Jekowsky
Alan Katz
Julie Larios
Irene Latham
Megan Litwin
Molly Lorenz
George Ella Lyon

J. David Martinez
Carmela A. Martino
Sara Matson
Rochelle Melander
Christy Mihaly
Amy Milholland
Kate McCarroll Moore
Kenn Nesbitt
Elisabeth Norton
Eric Ode
Abby Oqueli
Eric E. Peterson
Deborah Reidy
Laura Renauld
Joan Riordan
René Saldaña, Jr.
Michael Salinger
Darren Sardelli
Donna JT Smith
Eileen Spinelli
Elizabeth Steinglass
Lynn Street
Suma Subramaniam
Linda Picaro Tarantino
Pamela Taylor
Linda Jean Thomas
Joyce Uglow
Fernanda Valentino
Carol Varsalona
Padma Venkatraman
Charles Waters
April Halprin Wayland
Vicki Wilke
Allan Wolf
Janet Wong
Helen Kemp Zax
Darcy Day Zoells

EXERCISE #3: QUESTIONS

Keep a list of questions about things you wonder about.

Where Does The Sky Begin?

by Michael Salinger

Where does the sky begin?

I mean
what do you call the air a half inch above
a blade of grass?

Where does all that blue come from?

And why is it colder higher up
when you're actually closer to the sun?

11 Kinds of Clouds

cirrus
stratus
cumulus
nimbus
cirrostratus
cirrocumulus
altostratus
altocumulus
stratocumulus
nimbostratus
cumulonimbus

THIMBLETHOUGHT

The sun warms the ground and that heat rises, but as it does, it expands and loses warmth. It's called adiabatic heating.

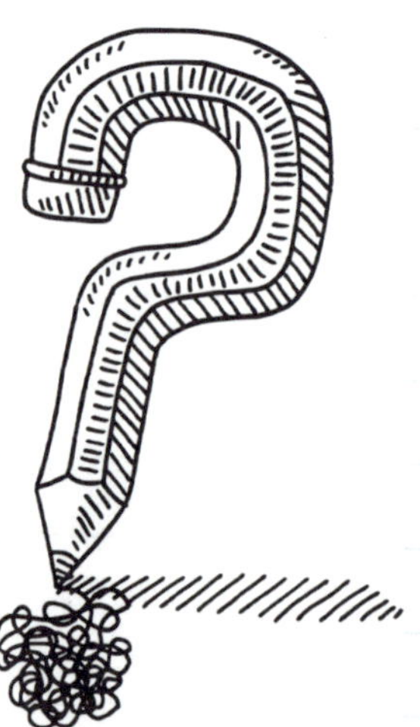

WONDERFUZZ

What does the sky look like to different animals?

THIMBLETHOUGHT

The question mark comes from the Latin word "quæstio," meaning "question," which was shortened to Qo with the capital Q written over the lowercase o, then evolving into the symbol we use today.

JUST WONDERING

by Christy Mihaly

Just wondering . . .
Why does water taste so wet?
Why do elephants never forget?
How tiny is the smallest dog?
What's the highest-jumping frog?
How do birds stay safe on wires?
Do you think a fly perspires?
Why do kiwi fruits have fuzz?
What makes bumblebees go "buzz"?
Why do dogs and babies drool?
Do all the teachers sleep at school?
Why do green lights mean you go,
while red is "stop," and yellow, "slow"?
And long ago, when you were small,
did you have traffic lights at all?

WONDERFUZZ

What do horses think about when they're standing in a field all day?

EXERCISE #4: WORD BANK

Make a list of words that are interesting to you. You can look them up in a dictionary and try using them in your writing.

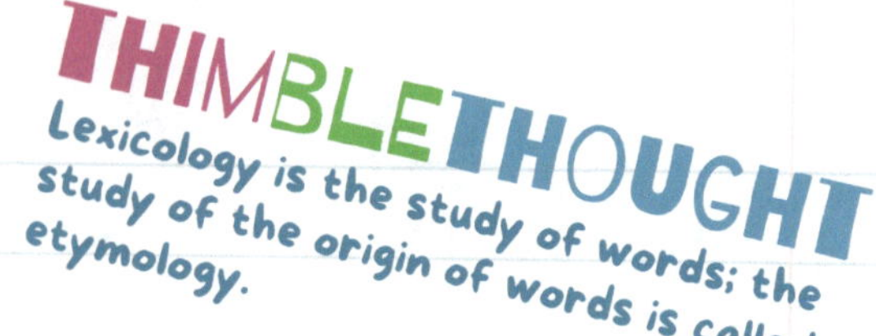

THIMBLETHOUGHT

Lexicology is the study of words; the study of the origin of words is called etymology.

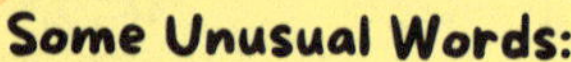

Some Unusual Words:
razzmatazz
gobbledygook
abracadabra
skedaddle
bumbershoot
hullaballoo
flabbergast

Words from Arabic:
apricot
coffee
hummus
sofa
sugar
algebra
chemistry

Words from German:
kindergarten
dachshund
pretzel
hamburger
gesundheit
wunderkind

Words from Japanese:
anime
manga
emoji
origami
sudoku
haiku

Words from Spanish:
alligator
avocado
barbecue
hurricane
mosquito
rodeo

Words from PETS!
woof - arf - bark
grrrrrrr - growl
meow - purr
squeak - chirp
tweet

WONDERFUZZ

Do machines have their own "machine language"?

This girl could be ME — CLARA!!!

The Wonder-er

by Irene Latham

There was a girl
who wondered things:
does a tree trunk ever
count its own rings?
She recorded her wonders
in an ordinary notebook.
On the cover she drew
a silvery fishhook
for snagging thimblethoughts
and wonderfuzz
and any not-ordinary words
that set her heart abuzz –
like *enigma, luminescent,*
gadzooks, and *effervescent.*
Each day more wonders,
each day more ink!
There was hardly time to think.
I wonder, the girl wrote,
beside the words *befuddled*
and *pondering . . .*
Is there such a thing
as too much wondering?

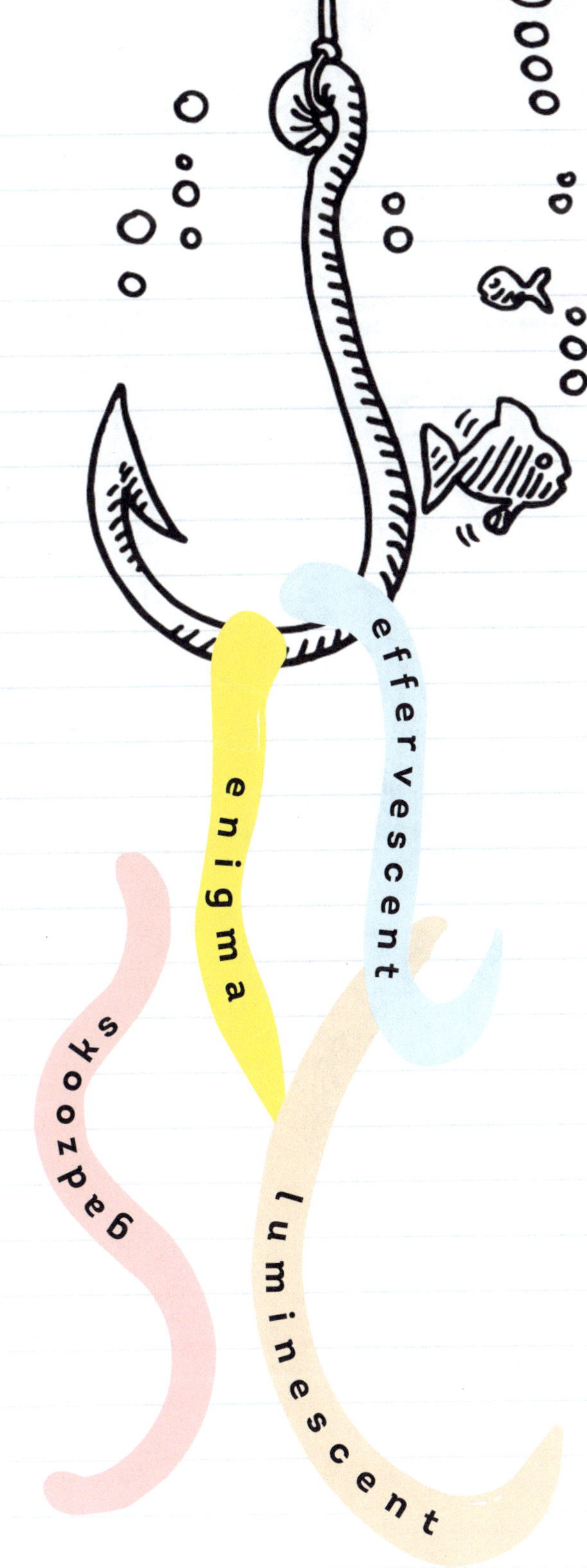

What is the longest word in the English language?

THIMBLETHOUGHT

The word "wonder" comes from the Old English word "wundor," which means "marvelous thing, the object of astonishment."

EXERCISE #5: FAMILY

Find pictures or drawings of some of your family members and write about them.

Everyone in my family
is equally important
but me and
my brother James and
my sister Vera and Mom —
and Uncle Frank (on Zoom) —
all know who is MOST important.
The rulers of our universe
(and living room)
are Rosie and
WOOF - WOOF - Wilby!

Me (Clara)

Uncle Frank

Mom
AKA Kristen

THIMBLE THOUGHT
In the United States a family consists of 3.13 people on average.

WONDERFUZZ
What is .13 of a person?

VERA
by Clara

V ery CUTE —
E verybody says so!
R eally smart
A nd kind, too!

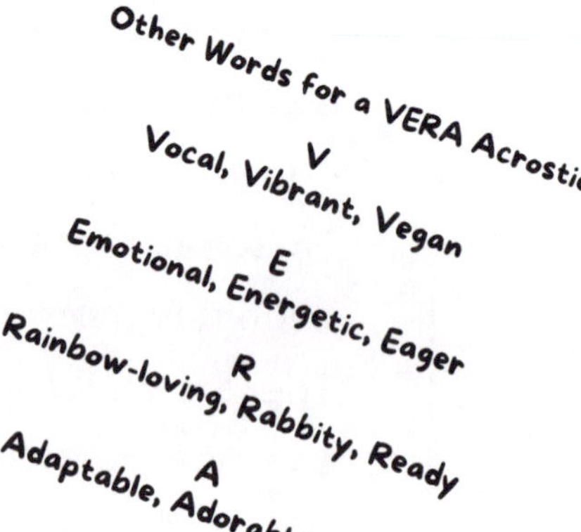

Other Words for a VERA Acrostic

V
Vocal, Vibrant, Vegan

E
Emotional, Energetic, Eager

R
Rainbow-loving, Rabbity, Ready

A
Adaptable, Adorable, Able

Rosie + Wilby

James

Vera

Mom's friend Julie (a PROFESSIONAL poet) wrote this funny poem four years ago when Vera was a little baby. We keep it on our refrigerator. Everyone should have a poem on their refrigerator!!

THIMBLETHOUGHT

Some people say that the order in which you are born affects your personality, so as a first-born, I might be a perfectionist.

THE BABY

by Julie Larios

Vera

Clara's very careful
With her younger brother James,
And James is very careful
With his younger sister, Vera,
And Vera's very . . . Vera's very . . .
Vera is . . . The Baby.

The Baby coos, The Baby smiles,
The Baby poops, The Baby pouts.
And does she wiggle, squeak and shout?
Does she ever! Vera!

James is pretty sure
He and Clara weren't babies
'Cuz
Babies can't say words, babies can't talk,
Babies have to learn to crawl
Before they learn to walk,
And James and Clara know they know
ALL there is to know, SO
Were they ever babies???? NO! NO! NO!

'Cuz Vera coos. Vera smiles.
Vera poops. Vera pouts.
Vera wiggles, squeaks and shouts.
Vera is a cutie pie . . .

Well, VERA IS THE BABY!

WONDERFUZZ

Is it true that baby seahorses ("fry") are completely independent as soon as they're born?

EXERCISE #6: PETS

Write about pets you have or have had — or wish you had.

AKA

by Joyce Uglow

I am
Anonymous
#IAmHereForTheDogs
#IAmAsCuteAsAPuppy
AKA James!

Clara's Favorite Dog Breeds

French bulldog
Labrador retriever
golden retriever
German shepherd
poodle
Shiba inu
mixed-breed hybrid/mutt
pug
Maltese
Border Collie

DOGS

by Patricia J. Franz

lean or chubby
lanky or squat
chill or a teeny bit crazy

scaredy or brave
unruly or trained
dainty or slightly slobbery

real food or kibble
sit still or wriggle
shaggy or beautifully groomed

silent or barky
at home or the park-y
I just want all the dogs

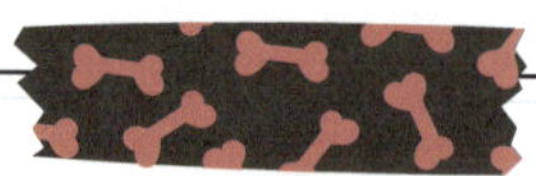

Antonyms or opposite word pairs:
lean, *chubby*
lanky, *squat*
chill, *crazy*
scaredy, *brave*
unruly, *trained*
dainty, *slobbery*
real food, *kibble*
sit still; *wriggle*
shaggy, *groomed*
silent, *barky*
at home, *park-y*

THIMBLETHOUGHT

There are about 400 dog breeds in the world, but 50% of the dogs in the U.S. are mixed-breed dogs.

WONDERFUZZ

Do dogs recognize each other as being "the same breed"?

THIMBLETHOUGHT

Basenji dogs are known as "barkless dogs" because they make so little noise, but they're not really mute. When they do decide to speak up, they make odd noises that sound like yodeling.

Everyone outside our family calls Wilby "Clara's dog" and calls our old Rosie "Mom's cat," but they are the bosses of us and we should be called THEIR people!

Clara's Dog

by David L. Harrison

Clara's dog is super silly.
Wilby is a real dilly,
a funny, goofball, willy-nilly –
until you hear him barking!

Wilby's barking shakes the ground.
Caterpillars for miles around
march in protest of the sound
of Wilby's monstrous barking.

Elephants shinny up a tree,
rhinos wheel about and flee,
lions cower, mew, and pee,
when they hear Wilby barking.

Wilby lives to have his fun.
He licks and loves on everyone,
but listen to what I'm saying, hon –
don't start Wilby barking!

WONDERFUZZ

I wonder if dogs bark in different dog languages, the way humans speak in different human languages?

Woof woof in Other Languages

Wuff wuff - German
Guau guau - Spanish
Wan wan - Japanese
Au au - Portuguese

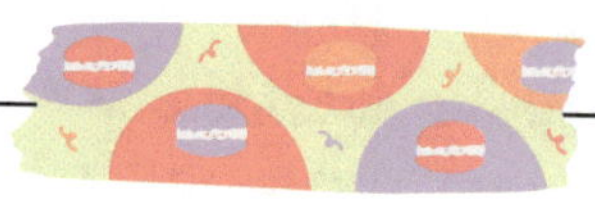

SIBLINGS

by Robyn Hood Black

Take the "r" out of brother, and what do you get?
BOTHER! That's what. He makes me upset.

Take the "i" out of sis, and what does it make?
"Ss" – like a hiss – the sound of a snake!

Please take them both, take them out of my sight.
Then I know everything will be all _ _ ght.

I said, everything will be all _ _ ght.
Hmmm.

Okay, please put back the "r," and return the "i," too –
I have to admit, I would miss those two.

Words that End in "g h t"

bright - fight
light - might
right - sight - tight
eight - height - weight
bought - fought - ought
straight

Do puppies miss their littermates after they're split up?

LAWS OF OUR FAMILY
by Clara
(with help from James + Vera + Mom)

Clean your plate.
Don't be late.
Keep your room clean.
Don't be mean.

No clothes on the floor.
Don't be a bore!
Slippers in the house.
No jumping on the couch!

No fighting. Share.
Show you care.
Be kind to each other —
ESPECIALLY YOUR MOTHER!

THIMBLETHOUGHT

Five ways to calm down are: breathe deeply, count to 10 slowly, take a walk, listen to music, and write down your feelings.

WONDERFUZZ

How are moles, scars, warts, scabs, and freckles like tattoos?

Popular Tattoos

heart - butterfly
rose - dragon
wings - star - skull
infinity sign
I love Daddy
I love Mom

I Know Mom Will Probably Say No But . . .

by Joan Riordan

I have a list of tattoos that I want.
The size. The pictures. The words. The font.
Animals. Vehicles. Instruments. Food.
Song lyrics. Idioms.
Something with mood.

My aunt's new ink is a wandering vine.
I ask my mom, "Can I ever get mine?"
"Of course, you can. Let's see your design.
That's perfect," she says –
"at age ninety-nine."

THIMBLE THOUGHT

It has been said that ancient Romans sometimes made tattoo ink from pine bark, vinegar, leeks, and . . . insect eggs!

"Mother" in Other Languages

Mutter (German)
Madre (Spanish)
Amma (Tamil)
Mère (French)
Omoni (Korean)
Mãe (Portuguese)
Al'umu (Arabic)
Maĭka (Bulgarian)

EXERCISE #7: NEIGHBORS

Write about some of your neighbors (or their pets).

James is complaining:
"99 is too old for my first tattoo!"
I remind him that our neighbor
three houses down,
Mr. Garcia,
is 99 years old
and in really good shape.
Mr. G. says he is going to live
to be 120 years old
so he can see us all graduate
from college.

Mr. G.'s dog Brisa
is Wilby's best (dog) friend.
Brisa eats only healthy food
EXCEPT when we give her cookies,
which she gobbles up
like a wild hurricane!

THIMBLETHOUGHT

Some things that centenarians (people who live to be 100 years old) have in common: daily exercise (even just walking or dancing a little), eating lots of vegetables, and spending time with people they like.

WONDERFUZZ

How old is the oldest living person in the world?

Free verse poems do not follow a set pattern or form and are usually irregular in line length. There can be some rhyming words scattered in a free verse poem, but there is not a regular pattern of rhyme.

List of Places Where People Live the Longest (Blue Zones)

Nicoya Peninsula, Costa Rica
Ikaria, Greece
Sardinia, Italy
Okinawa, Japan
Loma Linda, United States (California)

WONDERFUZZ

How do you train a dog to do math?

THIMBLETHOUGHT

The Border Collie descends from the sheepdog that was once found all over the British Isles.

PUPPY MATH

by Margarita Engle

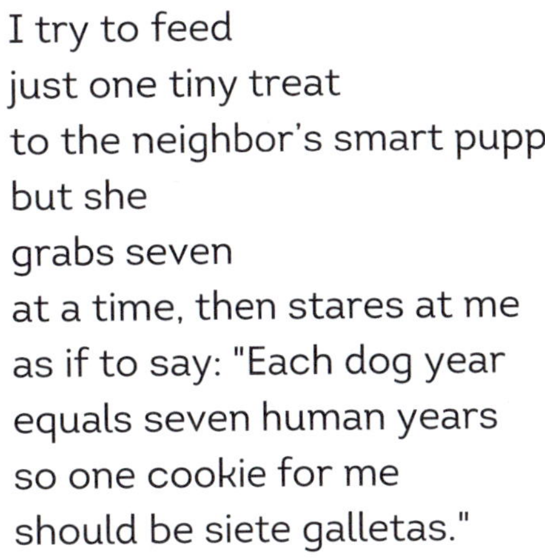

I try to feed
just one tiny treat
to the neighbor's smart puppy
but she
grabs seven
at a time, then stares at me
as if to say: "Each dog year
equals seven human years
so one cookie for me
should be siete galletas."

Border Collies are so intelligent
that even their 1 = 7 calculations
are bilingual.

free verse

7 Famous Math-Whiz Dogs

Luna the Mini Cockapoo
Maggie the Jack Russell
Mellie the Math Dog
Txoki (Alvaro Gonzalez Hernandez's dog)
Stewie the Scottish Terrier
Ruby the Dog Math Genius
Rae the French Bulldog

Uncle Frank (who lives in Germany) says that learning a second language makes your world bigger. Kids in our classroom know fifteen different languages: English, Spanish, German, Bulgarian, French, Portuguese, Arabic, Chinese, Japanese, Korean, Vietnamese, Hindi, Tamil, Tagalog, and Ukrainian. The world of our classroom keeps on growing!

Sumar Siempre Suma

por F. Isabel Campoy & Alma Flor Ada

Esta mano mía
tiene cinco dedos
y si miro, veo
que hay más todavía.
¡Qué casualidad
la otra es igual!
Y si miro, veo,
¡qué casualidad!
que tengo en un pie
cinco dedos más.
También en el otro.
Vamos a contar.
Cinco y cinco diez
arriba en las manos,
abajo en los pies . . .
¡Vamos a contar!
¿Cuántos dedos tengo
yo en total?

WONDERFUZZ

Do any other animals have fingerprints like human fingerprints?

THIMBLE THOUGHT

The fingerprints of koalas are similar to the fingerprints of humans.

8 Most Common Languages Spoken in the U.S.

English
Spanish
French
Chinese
Tagalog
Vietnamese
German
Arabic

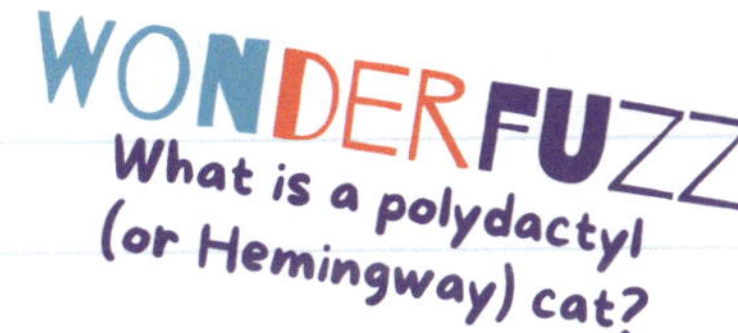

Adding Always Adds

by F. Isabel Campoy & Alma Flor Ada

On this hand of mine
I count five fingers.
Five more are on my other hand
and that, I think, is fine.
What a coincidence –
five on my left, five on my right!
But looking further,
what a coincidence!
I count five toes
on this foot of mine
and that, I think, is fine.
What a coincidence –
five on my left, five on my right!

Let's see how many
fingers and toes
I have in total.
Ten fingers up here,
ten toes down there.
Twenty in total
'cause adding always adds.

Kinds of Math

counting - estimating
addition
subtraction
multiplication
division
fractions
decimals
algebra
geometry
calculus

THIMBLETHOUGHT

If you walk about 8,000 steps a day, you'll walk over 100,000 miles in your lifetime, on average — that's enough to circle the globe four times!

EXERCISE #8: FRIENDS

Write about some of your friends (nearby or far away, "real" or "imaginary").

WONDERFUZZ
Is it possible to have too many friends?

I have school friends, neighborhood friends, sports friends, and friends who know me because of Mom and Uncle Frank. I'm putting Vera and James here in my friends circle too because you can be friends with your family, right?

THIMBLETHOUGHT
"A friend is someone who helps you up when you're down."
— Winnie-the-Pooh (A.A. Milne)

Vera

James

Elise

Bob

ME, Clara!

Amy

Sam

Jenny

Jane + Jade

THIMBLETHOUGHT

"A good friend is like a four-leaf clover: hard to find and lucky to have."
— Irish Proverb

Synonyms for Friend

bestie
buddy
chum
copilot
mate
pal
sidekick
BFF
blad

You're My Best Friend Forever

by Douglas Florian

You're my best friend forever.
Although we only met.
You're my best friend forever.
My favorite person yet.
You're my best friend forever.
My all-time favorite chum.
You're my best friend forever.
And our best is yet to come.
You're my best friend forever,
My buddy through and through.
You're my best friend forever.
You really are true blue.
You're my best friend forever.
You're in my hall of fame.
You're my best friend forever.

But I can't recall your name!

WONDERFUZZ

Are there tricks you can use to remember people's names?

THEY'RE THERE AGAIN?

by Clara

What's-his-name
said to What's-her-face,
"I seem to see you
all over the place!"

What's-her-face
looked in their mirror and said,
"We're the same person,
you Dodo-head!"

SPELL IT RIGHT!

they're = they are
there = a place
their = belongs to them

THE MORNING RUSH HAS MOM IN A TIZZY
by Clara

Mom told James to eat "quore mickly."
"Crack your backpack! Flush your hair!"
"Furry with your shoes!" she shrieked.
"And don't forget your . . . wonderwear!"

COWLICKED!

by Sara Matson

I have a cowlick on my head,
on top right near my crown –
a swirl where hair whirls up and left
and right, instead of down.

My mom attempts to spray it flat;
I push her hand away
hoping that the cow who licked
my head returns one day!

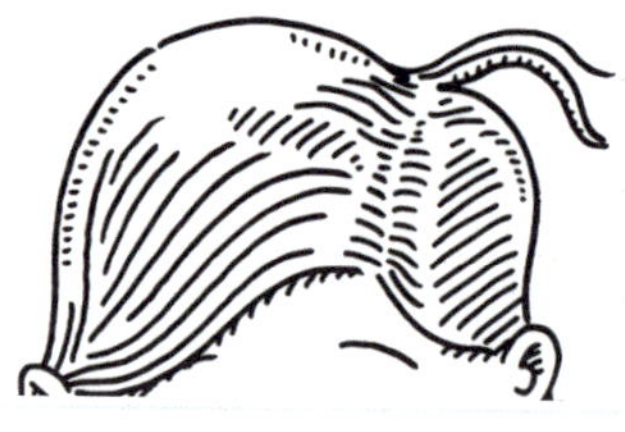

THIMBLETHOUGHT

ETYMOLOGY! The word "cowlick" comes from the 1500s and means a "tuft of hair that is out of position and natural direction," because it looks like a cow licked your head.

WONDERFUZZ

How long would a person's hair grow if they never EVER cut it (and lived to be 100 years old)?

WONDERFUZZ

Have people ever made shoes (completely) out of soft things like moss and feathers?

Kinds of Shoes

ballet flats
boat shoes
clogs
cowboy boots
flip-flops
galoshes
high-heeled
high-tops
hiking boots
light-up shoes
moccasins
mukluks
penny loafers
sandals
skate shoes
sneakers

Clara's Shoe Game

by Van G. Garrett

I have shoes that are squeaky.
Some overrun from too much fun.
Kicks that are kooky.
Sneakers brighter than the sun.

Animal prints and zig-zags.
Funky patterns – super-wild.
Laced art on canvases.
They all make me smile.

Except for when I have to make up my mind . . .
And I don't know what pair to wear.
And the eyes of too many soles are on me.
Wagging their tongues as they stare.

I go ahead, just make a choice. I look good and fresh!
I hope the World is ready for ME.
I'm SHOE GAME CLARA!
Smart. Pretty. And unique.

THIMBLETHOUGHT

Right and left shoes weren't available until 1817 when a cobbler in Philadelphia named William Young began making mirrored left/right shoes for his customers. (They became very popular!)

EXERCISE #9: GETTING TO SCHOOL

Do you walk to school? Ride the bus? Does someone drive you? Write about it.

GETTING THERE

by Alan Katz

When a parent drives you to school in the morning,
You get there very fast.
When you take the bus to school instead,
You'll find not much time has passed.
Walking to school takes longer,
And to me, the most fun of all
Is skipping the car and the bus and the walk
And hanging with friends as we
Crawl.

Will kids go to school someday on flying hoverboards?

THIMBLETHOUGHT

About 475,000 public school buses transport 25 million children to and from school and school-related activities every year.

THIMBLETHOUGHT

The phrase "jibber-jabber" is nearly 500 years old and is sometimes called "chitter-chatter" or "gibble-gabble."

Names that Start with J

Jenny, Joshua, Jason
Jack, Jing, Jessica
Jackie, Jordan, Jamal
Jade, Joseph, Julian
Jackson, Josephine, Juli
Jacob, Juan, Jane
Jonah, Jason, Jeremiah
Jasmine, Julius, Jolene
James, Jude, Juniper
Joon, Jalal, Justin

JIBBER-JABBER

by Janet Wong

Jenny and Johnny and Jason and I
like to hang out before school.
What did you watch on TV last night?
Those shoes are SUPER cool!
Mom says talking's a waste of time.
It's a bunch of useless blabber.
But we CANNOT start the day
without our jibber-jabber!

Say, "Hey!" Pay a compliment —
"Lilly, you're the BEST!"
Then point out things you've noticed:
"You're so clever — I'm impressed!"

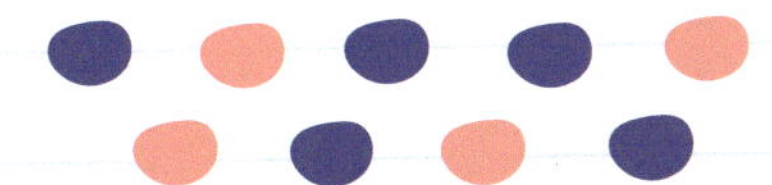

HARRY HAS A CELL PHONE
by Clara

The photographer's fancy new camera
had an AI malfunction inside.
Grins became grimaces, faces froze,
and a beard appeared on Ms. Hyde.
The photographer's tricks didn't fix things.
AI has a mind of its own.
But Picture Day was saved in the end —
thanks to a fourth grader's phone.

4TH GRADE TEACHERS
MERGELER ELEMENTARY

THIMBLE THOUGHT

When you take a digital photo, you capture the date and time and even the GPS coordinates for the location of the photo.

BREAKING INTO A SMILE
by Clara

I was feeling kind of blue
but I put on my happy face.
My smile was a mile wide —
from Earth to outer space!

Taking school photos started in 1922. Each photo cost 10 cents or 6 photos for fifty cents!

SCHOOL PHOTO DAY

by Avis Harley

There's an air of excitement through the hallway.
A photographer has come to our school today!

Each class is called, one by one,
down to the gym where the photos are done.

The photographer likes to place us by height,
getting us children to look just right.

"Tall ones behind,
Small ones in front,
Mediums all together!"

When we've settled down and the picture's complete,
we return to our class, and I repeat:

"Tall ones behind,
Small ones in front,
Mediums all together!"

Which of these friends, I wonder,
will I always have
forever?

Famous Friends

Mario + Luigi
Frodo + Samwise
Sherlock + Dr. Watson
Barbie + Ken
Olaf + Sven
Buzz + Woody
Charlotte + Wilbur
Elephant + Piggie
Frog + Toad
Sylvia + Janet!!

WONDERFUZZ

What is most important (for determining your height): sleep, food, exercise, or genetics?

EXERCISE #10: FAVORITE FOOD
Do you have a favorite food (at school or at home)? Write about it.

THIMBLETHOUGHT

Research shows that students who eat breakfast or lunch at school get more whole grains, milk, fruits, and vegetables and have a healthier diet at school.

CLARA'S GOT THE LUNCHIE MUNCHIES

by Charles Waters

Lunchie Munchie
yum, yum, yum,
I gobble, gobble
every crumb.

Tofu turkey,
vegan cheese,
lettuce, olives,
onions, peas.

Carrots, celery,
hummus dip,
my favorite cookie –
chocolate chip!

I gobble, gobble
every crumb.
Lunchie Munchie
yum, yum, yum.

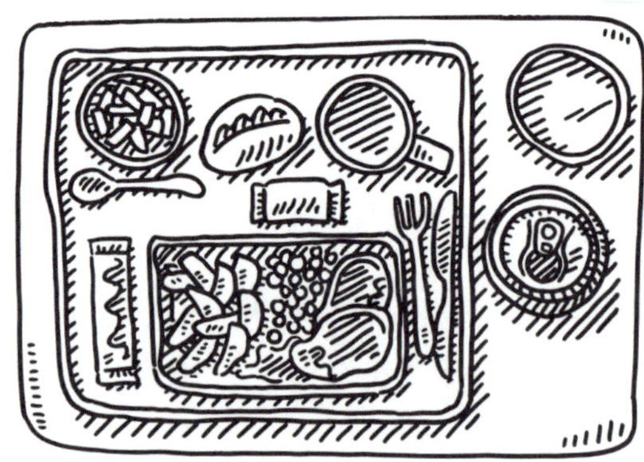

POINTER

by Helen Kemp Zax

If you give your mouse a cookie
or share crumblings of that ilk –
your keyboard will be grateful
if you skip the glass of milk.

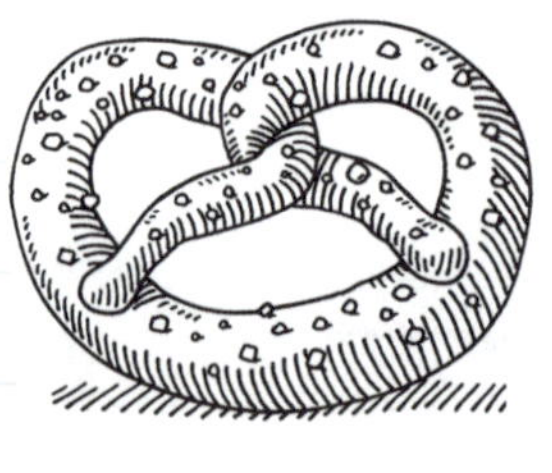

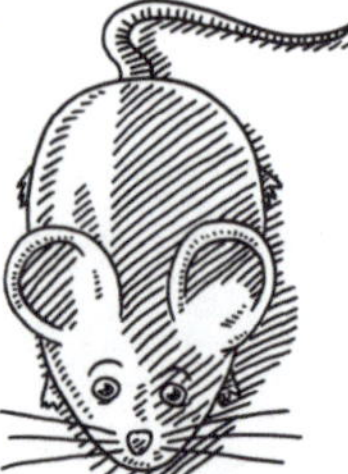

WONDERFUZZ

Can you be vegan (eat nothing from animals, not even milk or eggs or honey) and still grow tall and strong?

THIMBLETHOUGHT

A flute made from a vulture's bones is the world's oldest musical instrument.

Lunchroom Virtuosos

by Allan Wolf

Vickie is a virtuoso
of the pickle flute.
She puckers on her piccolo [pickle-o]
with trills and tweets and toots.

Victor is a virtuoso
of the juice-box drum.
Carrot-sticking steady tempo,
loudly popping gum.

Val's a virtuoso of
the broccoli sitar.
And I'm a virtuoso
of the ham-and-cheese guitar.

We're brilliant virtuosos,
but our teacher says we're rude.
It seems what we call "music,"
she calls, "Playing with your food."

Assonance (the repetition of the same vowel sound) – the short /i/ sound: *Vickie, pickle, piccolo, trill.*
Consonance (the repetition of the same consonant sound) – the /k/ sound in: *pickle, puckers, piccolo, pickle-o;* the /l/ sound in: *pickle, flute, piccolo, trills.*

Musical Instrument Families

percussion
woodwind
strings
brass
keyboard

WONDER FUZZ

What are the weirdest things that musicians use to make music?

EXERCISE #11: WORRIES
Are there things (big or small) you worry about? Write about it.

Mrs. Booker says
a test is a chance
to show the world what you can do.
It's like a sports game.

If you don't do your best, no worries!
Another chance will come around.
You can do better next time.
No one makes EVERY shot.
Mrs. Booker says
my favorite basketball players,
LeBron James and Caitlin Clark,
actually miss HALF their shots.

If that's true, I might be on track
to become the G.O.A.T.
of test-taking!

TEST DREAD

by Kate McCarroll Moore

Gosh!
Good grief!
Yikes! Stripes! Wow!
Oh, no!
Oy vey!
Oh, rats!
Not now!
This is what I want
To say
When I find out
It's pop quiz day.

"G.O.A.T." or "GOAT" is an acronym for "Greatest of All Time." It probably started with hip-hop music in the 1990s, and then LL Cool J made it popular.

7 Lucky Things to Do Before a Test

Eat something red at breakfast
Wear something white or blue
Wash your hands backwards
Jump 10 times on each foot
Hum a happy song
Make a giraffe neck
DESKERCISE!

Is it true that a giraffe's neck holds up to 600 pounds?

Mrs. Booker loves to share test-taking tips. She put these pointers on a poster in the front of the room.

TEST-TAKING TIPS
for Champions

STAY CALM.
You can handle this test.

CONCENTRATE.
And you'll do your best.

SET YOUR OWN PACE.
Not too fast, not too slow.

CHECK YOUR WORK.
Did you show what you know?

FEEL THE FLOW.
It's like playing a game.

YOU CAN HANDLE THIS TEST.
Just use your brain!

WONDERFUZZ
Are there any schools where they have NO tests?

THIMBLETHOUGHT
Children were not required to go to school until after 1880. Many children worked in factories with their parents instead.

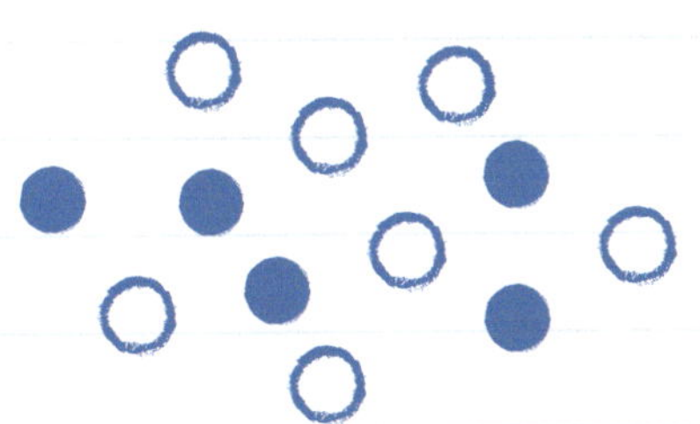

EXERCISE #12: MATH INTERSECTIONS

Write about something you've learned about in math this year.

by Carmela A. Martino

Back in 1557, mathematician Robert Recorde
grew weary with writing "is equal to"
over and over and over again
in his math equations.
So he designed a new notation –
a pair of perfectly parallel lines –
now known as
the equal sign.

Surprisingly, use of his invention
did not multiply in Recorde's lifetime.
But everyone knows the sequel
to the story of the equal sign:
over time, its usage climbed,
and climbed, and climbed,
and is today . . .
unequaled.

WONDERFUZZ

Does playing chess make you better at math?

THIMBLE THOUGHT

Math comes in handy for planning travel costs, understanding car loans, following sports stats, cooking meals, treating illnesses, and more.

NOTE: Mathematician Robert Recorde introduced the equal sign in his 1557 math book, *The Whetstone of Witte*. The strange title is a pun that basically means "an algebra book on which to sharpen one's mathematical wit." Unfortunately, Recorde died the year after the book's publication, and the equal sign wasn't used in print again until 1618. In some places, the custom of writing out the words "is equal to" in mathematical equations persisted into the 1700s.

Math Words to Remember

product
the answer to a multiplication problem

difference
the answer to a subtraction problem

quotient
the answer to a division problem

sum
the answer to an addition problem

If you start with a penny and double its value every day, how much money will you have in one month?

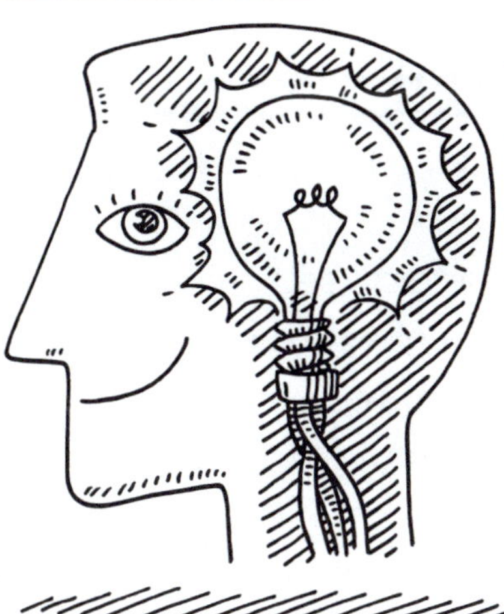

STUPID
by Clara

I feel stupider
than a hundred hedgehogs,
more stupid than a gnat.
I think my brain fell out
at recess, hit the ground,
and . . . SPLAT.

JUMBLE OF NUMBERS
by Mary E. Cronin

In math class, I'm lost in a jumble of numbers.
I grumble and struggle with quotients and sums.
My face gets hot, my heartbeat drums
as my brain churns
and burns
and hums.
This tangle of numbers . . . I try to un-knot it.
Wait, wait, hold up!
Boom –
I got it!

The word "hundred" comes from the old Norse term "hundrath," which actually means 120 and **not** 100.

A "jiffy" is an actual unit of time. It means 1/100th of a second.

EXERCISE #13: SCIENCE EXPLORATIONS

Write about something you've learned about in science this year.

ROBOT

by Jane Heitman Healy

I made myself a robot clone,
I thought he'd come in handy.
He'd go to school in place of me.
Now wouldn't that be dandy?

I programmed him to move and speak
And sit still in the classroom,
While I stayed home and played Fortnite
And met with friends on Zoom.

It worked just fine until the day
He had to take a test.
We got an "F." Without a brain,
He couldn't do his best.

Things I Wish a Robot Could Do

Clean my room
Take my tests
Pick up dog poop
Babysit my sister
Cook dinner
Do my homework
Forecast the weather
Eat my broccoli
Scare away bullies
Fix my bicycle

Is it true that the first robot was invented more than 1,500 years ago?

THIMBLETHOUGHT

Leonardo Da Vinci designed a human-like robot in 1464. His robot was called the "mechanical knight," and it could move its arms, sit, and stand.

WONDERFUZZ

If you could build a robot that would eat your vegetables, how would it "clean itself out"?

My Robot Is Awesome!

by Kenn Nesbitt

I built this cool robot
for homework today.
My robot is awesome!
It does what I say!

It washes the dishes.
It vacuums the floors.
It takes out the garbage.
It does ALL my chores.

It likes to bake cookies.
It plays games with me.
My robot is awesome!
You have to come see!

There's only one thing that
I WISH it would do . . .
But sadly, it won't eat
my vegetables too.

Mrs. Booker told us to find a MENTOR TEXT to inspire us. I used this mentor text.

MY ROBOT

by Clara

My robot does homework.
My robot does chores.
Thanks to my robot,
I never get bored.
My robot bakes cookies.
My robot is handy.
My robot can even
poop out rainbow candy!
My robot can guess
whatever I feel.
Huh? What did you say?
My robot's not real?!
Well, I guess . . .
I have homework.
Let's get sprockets and gears.
I ought to be finished . . .
in about fifty years!

Repetition (repeating words, lines, phrases) adds interest, music, and **fun** to a poem!

THIMBLE THOUGHT

The word "robot" was coined by a Czech writer and comes from the Czech word "robota," which means "forced labor."

EXERCISE #14: AFTER SCHOOL
What do you like to do AFTER school? Write about it.

PIRATE
by Deborah Reidy

The pirate was having trouble.
He couldn't read or write.
He was trying his best to learn those things.
He studied every night.

The pirate was good with numbers.
He could count to thirty-three,
but when he tried to recite the alphabet,
he kept getting lost at C!

THIMBLE THOUGHT

Until the 1900s the word "homework" meant "work done at home" (not in a shop or factory) and was not related to schoolwork.

WONDERFUZZ

If "piece of cake" means "easy," what kind of food would mean "hard"?

Synonyms are words with the same meaning like: ***easy, simple, nothing to it,*** and ***"piece of cake."***

HOMEWORK
by Deborah Reidy

"It will be easy," said Clara's teacher.
"It's so simple," said her brother.
"Nothing to it," added her father.
"I agree," nodded her mother.

So Clara quickly did her homework
without taking a break.
And then she happily ate it,
since it was a piece of cake!

Mom says: "Would you like to play video games? Then it's time for homework: JUST. GET. IT. DONE!"

You know what rocks? Kaleidoscope socks!!

Behind The Hidden Door

by Darren Sardelli

We opened a door to a magical world
where pumpkins are silver and blue.
The moon in the sky was a strawberry pie.
Bananas were shaped like a Q.
A monkey was wearing kaleidoscope socks.
Pianos had candy cane keys.
A mouse with a moustache was zooming around
in a bright yellow car made of cheese.

Vanilla volcanoes had pudding-filled tops
that bubbled in blueberry rain.
We noticed a pig in pistachio pants.
A hippo was flying a plane.
Invisible bunnies left tracks in the snow.
Identical horses were neighing.
We all were amazed by these things that we saw
in this video game we were playing.

This poem is full of **alliteration** with repeated consonant sounds at the beginning of many words. Some examples of adjacent alliterative words include: ***candy cane, vanilla volcanoes, pistachio pants.***

Other alliterative words that are simply near each other include: ***mouse/moustache, bubbled/blueberry, pig/pistachio.***

THIMBLETHOUGHT

Tetris was the first video game played in space — by Russian astronaut Aleksandr A. Serebrov.

My cousin Joanne came up with an idea for a Bunk-a-munka video game. She even wrote a song for it. I think her funky game will make her rich and FAMOUS!

WONDERFUZZ

Could a kid make money from writing lyrics for really silly songs?

I Met a Funky Monkey

by Joanne Emery

I met a funky monkey,
In the pale moonlight.
He had a peacock's tail
And his eyes were shining bright.

I followed funky monkey,
And we sang a silly song:

Funk-a-munka,
Hunk-a-munka,
Bunk-a-munka-moo.

Me-a-munka,
You-a-munka.
Toodle-loodle-loo!

We chattered and we chanted,
We stomped along the road,
We did the cha-cha and the rumba
Till we met a purple toad.

We laughed when we saw him,
We were happy as could be,
We danced in the moonlight,
And sailed off on the sea.

The boat rocked, rolled, and rumbled,
A serpent rose from the foam,
And with his mighty breath,
He blew us all back home.

Funk-a-munka,
Hunk-a-munka.
Bunk-a-munka-moo.

Me-a-munka,
You-a-munka.
Toad-a-loada-loo!

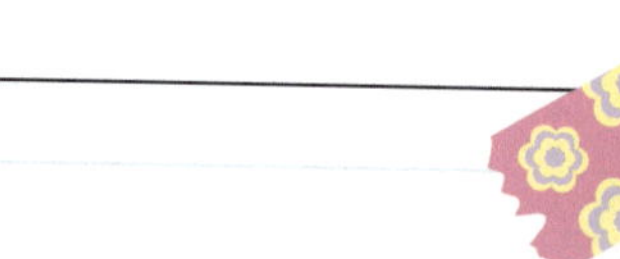

7 a.m.: wake up (UGH - too early)
8 a.m. to 3 p.m.: School
3:30 p.m.: Snacks + sports
5 p.m.: Dinner
6 p.m.: Homework + chores
7 p.m.: Fun + games
8 p.m.: Bath/shower + reading
9 p.m.: Time to sleep + DREAM!

Sweet Sixteen

by George Ella Lyon

Rosie dozes
on my shoulder,
in my lap
bony old girl,
tortoiseshell fur
coming off
in tufts.

At night
she waits
in the hall
for me
to prepare
her favorite
drink:

bathwater
with me
in it.

WONDERFUZZ

Is it better for your health to take a bath or a shower?

THIMBLETHOUGHT

In 1883, John Michael Kohler invented the world's first bathtub by taking a cast-iron horse trough, adding four decorative feet to the bottom, and covering it in enamel.

WONDERFUZZ

Do the people and things I see in my dreams live in another world when I'm awake?

DREAMS

by Merry Bradshaw

Dreams
Creep
Sneak
Zig
    and
        zag

LARGE
Small
Round or tall

Giant castles
Barking dogs
Dancing dragons
Big red frogs
Squirrels on scooters
Fish in trees
Owls in hammocks
    watching
        bees

Wild
Crazy
Creatures new

They find their way
to
sleeping
YOU

Common Dream Themes

being chased
being naked in public (!)
falling
flying
going to the bathroom
losing teeth
seeing old friends
running
swimming
taking a test

gute nacht = good night (in German)

THIMBLETHOUGHT

In the field of psychology, the subfield of oneirology (oh-ny-rology) is the scientific study of dreams.

THIMBLE THOUGHT

Sometimes
(before I fall asleep)
I think about
what I want to see
in my dreams . . .
and
every once in a while
it works!!!

ELEPHANTASY

by Jane Heitman Healy

I heard a herd of elephants.
They tromped right past my door
And headed toward the deep blue sea,
A thousand miles or more.

I wonder if they got there,
If their bodies liked to float,
If their trunks were meant for swimming
Or if they used a boat.

I like to think about them.
Are they having fun?
Ears stretched out beside their heads,
Soaking in the sun.

WONDERFUZZ

Is it true that elephants spend up to 18 hours a day EATING?

Elephant Facts

Elephants are very smart.
They eat 200–600 pounds of food each day.
Females (matriarchs) rule.
They can use their trunks like snorkels when they swim.
They can use vibrations to speak.
They can listen through the bones in their feet.

EXERCISE #15: WORD HUNT

Write a poem that uses homophones or homographs or any kind of wordplay.

LANGUAGE ARTS

WONDERFUZZ

How can horses grow to be so fast and strong when all they eat is grass and hay?

Horses have excellent hearing: they can rotate their ears 180 degrees and detect sounds in different directions.

homophone = two words that sound the same but have different spellings and meanings

Nay

by Donna JT Smith

My horse does not talk –
not even a whisper!
Perhaps it's just hoarse;
can't speak any crisper.

Some say its voice
is as clear as a bell;
it won't whinny "yes,"
but "nay" it neighs well!

But, hey . . .
you'll never hear nay
to eating some hay!
No weigh . . . whoops!
No way!

The HORSE is HOARSE!
Hay - hey!
No way —
no weigh!!
I love homophones!!

Horace (Who Is a Horse) Is Hungry.

by Jay Brazeau

So, I bought a
ten-pound sack of oats
but Horace said,
"Nope, take a note –
I'd really prefer
a handful of hay
or half an apple
or a carrot,
okay?
It's not as much food,
but they get my vote –
those oats, I'm afraid,
don't float my boat."

homograph = two words that are spelled the same but have different sounds and meanings

WONDERFUZZ

Is it true that some ants, termites, and beetles are "fungus farmers" who grow their own food?

Here's the mentor text for my poem FULL of homographs + homophones, too!

HOW NOW BROWN SOW
by Clara

How now brown sow?
What will you sow over there?
They're seeds for wheat?
Hooray! Soon we'll eat
fresh-baked bread every day!

But the wind is strong;
if you plant the seeds wrong
we'll wind up without any crops.
And the piglets we bred
will go hungry instead
of feasting on toast
in their slops!

A Sow's Vow
by Sara Matson

Once upon a fertile farm
there lived a stylish sow
who always wore her fancy clothes
when she went out to plow.

In gauzy gown with beaded bows
she'd sow the corn and wheat,
driving up and down the rows
with diamond-studded feet.

But one day, after thunderstorms
had turned her fields to mud,
she slipped – her shoe caught on the plow –
and fell down with a THUD.

Head bowed in thought, the soiled sow
sat propped against the wheels.
"After this," she vowed aloud,
"I'll never plow in heels!"

THIMBLETHOUGHT

Miss Piggy, Porky Pig, Peppa Pig, Wilbur, Piglet, Babe, and Pumbaa are just a few of the famous pigs from stories, movies, and television.

My Teacher Has a Fish Tank TV

by Amy Milholland

My teacher has a fish tank TV.
It used to be just a TV,
but then he put a fish tank in it.
I ask him,
"Why do you have a fish tank TV?"
He says to me, "I had an old TV,
and I like fish.
Plus, they're a school of fish,
so I thought
they'd like to come to school with me!"
Then I wonder,
What would a school of fish do at school?
Would they study English and math?
After gym, would they need to take a bath,
since they're already wet?
Do fish even sweat?

THIMBLETHOUGHT

People sometimes repurpose old vintage televisions into shelves, a drink caddy, a dog bed, a puppet theater, or a play kitchen!

WONDERFUZZ

When ships sink to the bottom of the sea, do fish play with the stuff they find inside?

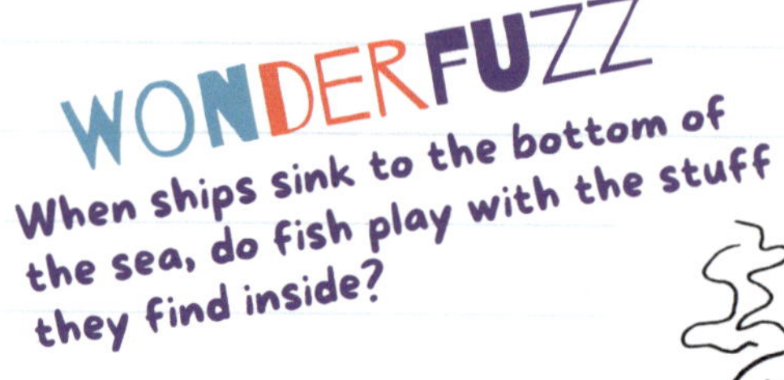

Groups of Animals

SCHOOL of fish
CAULDRON of bats
CLOWDER of cats
PARADE of elephants
PRICKLE of porcupines
TOWER of giraffes
LEAP of leopards
POD of whales
PRIDE of lions
ROMP of otters
PACK of wolves
CRASH of rhinos

PORCUPINE MATH (an equation poem)
by Clara

A feisty leap of leopards + a prickle of porcupines = A zillion x OUCH!!!

WONDERFUZZ

are there any famous writers who never use capital letters or punctuation

free
by Clara

no
caps
no
punctuation
i
can
write
any
way
i
want
in
a
poem

So many **apostrophes**! I'm (seven times),
You'd, haven't, you're, Don't, Could've, should've.
Plus **possessive apostrophes:**
Clara's, brother's, parents'.

THIMBLETHOUGHT

In an "apostrophe poem" the poet speaks to an animal or object or thing that cannot talk back.

MIGHTY APOSTROPHE

by Fernanda Valentino

I'm teeny, tiny, really small.
You'd hardly notice me at all.

Eating letters is one thing I do,
Which means a bit less work for you.

If you haven't noticed, look carefully.
I'm powerful! I'm mighty! Apostrophe!

I'm hiding in you're,
And in "Don't fall!"
Could've, and should've,
But that isn't all –

I'm also possessive of
Clara's glove,
My brother's bike,
And my parents' love.

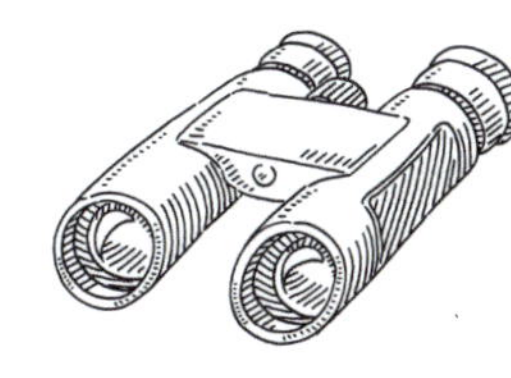

I'm in so many places! Go and look.
Come find me! I'm hiding inside this book!

THIMBLETHOUGHT #53

by Irene Latham

If I could live forever
and you would be with me
I'd choose a million books
and snuggle inside a library.

EXERCISE #16: WILD ANIMALS
Make a list of wild animals.
Find a poem and 3 or more facts about one you choose.

ANIMAL REPORTS

GROUP WORK

We're spending our RAW time (Research and Writing time) today doing the BRAINSTORMING for a group report that is due next week. Our first step is to come up with a list of animals. Then we need to find a poem and find facts about each animal. So far we have:

- ✓ PENGUIN
- ✓ SQUID
- ✓ MANATEE
- ✓ CAT
- ✓ PARROT
- ✓ WORM
- ✓ CATERPILLAR
- ✓ CHICKEN
- ✓ DINOSAUR
- ✓ OSTRICH

THIMBLETHOUGHT

Wild animals find their own food and shelter and do not need humans to survive. Domestic animals live with humans as pets or on farms.

WONDERFUZZ

Why would any animal want to be wild during the dark, cold winter (instead of living in a warm and cozy barn)?

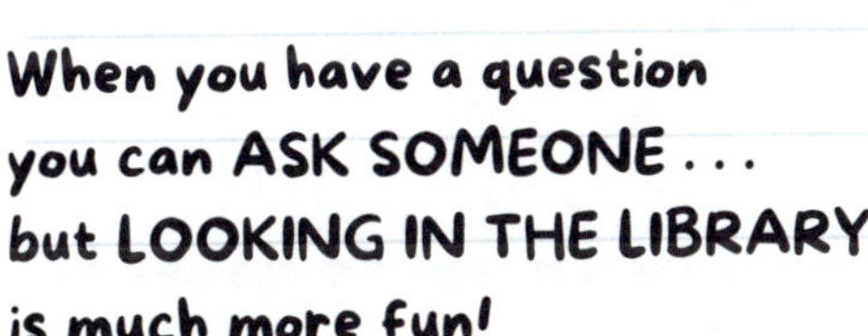

RESEARCH
by Clara

When you have a question
you can ASK SOMEONE . . .
but LOOKING IN THE LIBRARY
is much more fun!

A librarian will show you
shelves where you should look.
You can even borrow
a tall tower of books.

Or type some keywords and
do a SEARCH IN GOOGLE
such as:
What's the difference,
trumpet versus bugle?

Many websites will pop up
that talk about the shape
and how the two are used
and the sounds that they make.

But my teacher says
be smart. Read closely. Beware:
there are so many
misleading sources out there.

There are websites that
simply cannot be trusted.
If you aren't careful,
YOU. WILL. BE. BUSTED!

THIMBLE THOUGHT

If something can be proven, it is a fact. If it is only your opinion or others can agree or disagree with it, it's fiction.

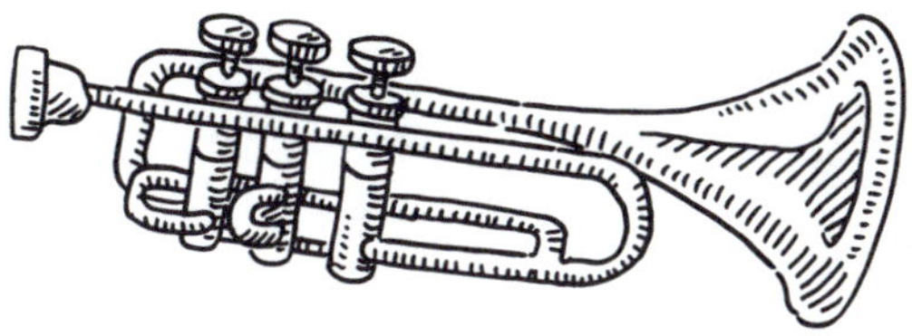

WONDERFUZZ

Why are grown-ups always arguing about whether the news is fake or real?

African gray parrots live in the rainforests of central and western Africa. They are prized as pets because of their extraordinary ability to mimic human speech.

YACKETY-YACKER

by Helen Kemp Zax

The African Gray is a fancy, fast talker –
a squealer, a shrieker, a squeaker, a squawker,
a yipper, a yapper, a yelper, a yowler,
a rumbler, a grumbler, a howler, a growler.
At home in his forest this mimicking cackler
will never be caught saying, "I want a cracker."

Jade and Jane picked the African Gray Parrot.

WONDERFUZZ

Can a parrot learn to read?

Famous Cartoon Birds

Road Runner
Tweety Bird
Donald Duck
Daffy Duck
Big Bird
Woodstock (Peanuts)
Zazu (Lion King)
Kevin (Up)
Blu (Rio)
Iago (Aladdin)
Owl (Winnie the Pooh)

THIMBLETHOUGHT

Parrots are the only animals in the world that can mimic human speech — they can even sing opera!

I picked cats. Amy says we can only write about WILD animals and a cat doesn't count. Amy doesn't know how WILD our cat Rosie can be!

If a cat blinks slowly at you, it means they love you!

Rosie says, ROAR!
I caught one mouse but I want many, MANY more!!

WILD

by Laura Renauld

Do not be fooled by my bowl of food.
I am wild.
I crouch in wait for prey to come my way.

I am as still as stone.
My ears may twitch and my eyes will dart,
but they do not count.
So what if my tail has a mind of its own?
I am as still as stone.

The prey! It comes my way . . .

Straight shot – paw swat – prey caught.
Do not be fooled by my felt mouse or my snug house.
I am wild.

Domestic cats communicate with several "vocalizations" including purring, trilling, hissing, growling, snarling, and many different forms of meowing.

Why do we call some animals "wild animals," but we don't use those words for other animals (like Rosie)?

THIMBLETHOUGHT

Vampire squids have glowing tips at the end of their 8 arms to scare away enemies — and their arms grow back if they're lost or eaten.

VAMPIRE-ISH

by Linda Jean Thomas

How did the vampire squid get its name?
Does it always say,
"I *vant* to drink your blood!"?
No, never, no way!
It doesn't hunt live prey in the sea.
Instead, it eats dead animal debris.
But with its vampire-ish cloak
of spikey, webbed arms,
this squid evades predators
that would do it harm!

Amy's choice

The vampire squid lives deep in the ocean where the water is cold and there is no sunshine and little oxygen. They are red or black and the size of a football with huge eyes. They feed on "marine snow" (dead matter).

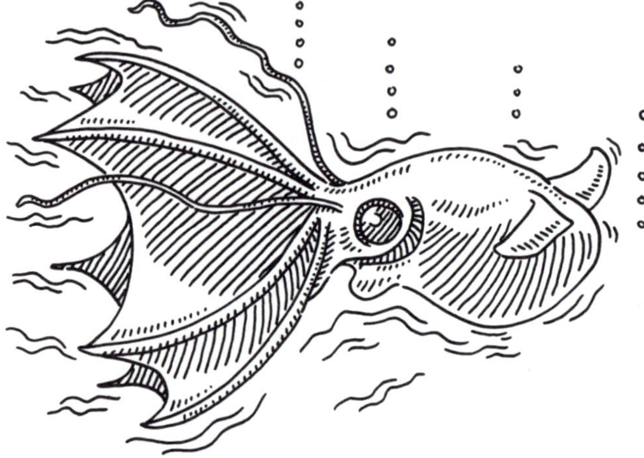

Ocean's Weirdest Creatures

Leafy Sea Dragon
Christmas Tree Worm
Anglerfish
Northern Stargazer
Red Handfish
Wobblegong
Sea Pig
Bloodbelly Comb Jelly
Japanese Spider Crab
Gulper Eel
Blobfish
Goblin Shark

WONDERFUZZ

How do animals know when their food is spoiled? (There's no expiration date stamped on food in nature!)

WONDERFUZZ

Do animals consider some animals "more beautiful" than others?

THIMBLETHOUGHT

The term "decorator crab" describes many different crabs, including several different species of spider crabs, harlequin crabs, moss crabs, little seaweed crabs, and toothed crabs.

OUTERWEAR

by Elisabeth Norton

For the Underwater Fashion Show
I've got the perfect thing to wear:
My shell – a masterpiece of art,
Unique and full of flair.
With seaweed, shells, and sponges
All placed with utmost care
I'll strut right down the runway
And all the fish will stare!

Sam's choice

Note: Decorator crabs collect items that they attach to thin hooks on their shells. Scientists believe they do this as a camouflage or defense against predators. When they shed their old shell, many decorator crabs recycle their old decorations from their old shell, moving them carefully to the new shell as it hardens.

Kinds of Crabs

- Fiddler crab
- Chinese mitten crab
- Tasmanian giant crab
- Shore crab
- Florida stone crab
- Ghost crab
- Giant mud crab
- Japanese spider crab
- Dungeness crab
- Snow crab
- Chesapeake blue crab
- King crab

THIMBLETHOUGHT

Many dinosaurs had feathers, the largest being the Yutyrannus Huali, a super predator and cousin of T-Rex.

CHICKENOSAURUS

by Rochelle Melander

I'm king of the coop.
Chip off the block.
You can see it in my waddle,
you can hear it in my squawk!
I'm a star, I'm a stud,
I've got T-Rex in my blood.
Hear me rumble!
Hear me roar!
Grandma was a dinosaur.

Bob has chosen a "chickenosaurus."
What on earth is THAT?!

Mythical Creatures

Golem
Oni
Cyclops
Ogre
Loch Ness Monster
Gnome
Fairy
Bigfoot
Chimera
Hydra
Zombie
Banshee
Dybbuk
Vampire
Mermaid
Dragon

WONDERFUZZ

Are birds really related to dinosaurs?

A "portmanteau" (port-man-**toe**) is a word that blends parts of two words along with their meanings into one word, like "brunch," which combines "breakfast" and "lunch."

A TERROR OF TYRANNOSAURS

by Clara

The first T-rex stands above me.
A second sits perched below.
A third one squats beside me.
A fourth one hides in a hole.
Behind me there's a fifth one.
It's heading toward my head.
Good thing they're only statues
and the real-life ones are dead!

Fun Facts about Eggs

The average American eats about 286 eggs per year.

Iowa produces the most eggs in the US.

Eggs are good for your eyes. Eggs contain antioxidants and brain nutrients.

Hard-boiled eggs spin easily, raw eggs wobble.

More than 99% of animals lay eggs.

Eggs bought in grocery stores will never hatch.

Now Bob is going to pick a regular chicken so we will stop our squawking about the made-up chickenosaurus . . .
EXCEPT
Elise is complaining that it is not a wild animal.

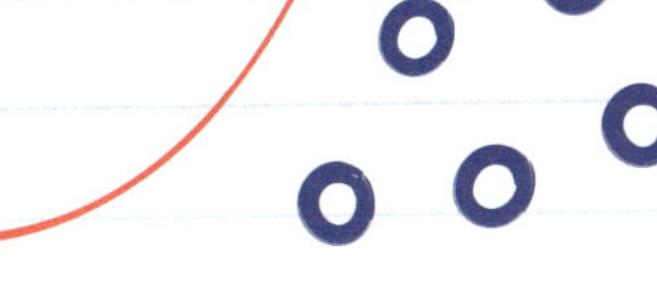

A Chicken Can't Be Picky

by Kristy Dempsey

A chicken eats by picking up
wee pecks from off the ground.
She clucks about while pecking up
the picks that she has found.
She does not bother checking on
the pieces for their flavor.
A chicken pecks just what she picks
with little time to savor.
For if the hen is choosy
or selective in her picks,
she just might find her pecks were picked
by not so picky chicks.

Chickens have their own society and know their "pecking order" within the group. They have good memories and even dream when they sleep. They eat seeds and grains, but bugs and mice, too.

THIMBLETHOUGHT

Chickens actually have a good memory for faces and can remember about 100 different faces.

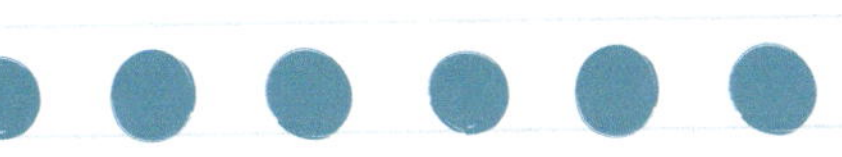

THIMBLETHOUGHT

Ostriches are the fastest running birds in the world, running at speeds up to 40 mph. They can cover 10 feet in a single stride.

WONDERFUZZ

Do ostriches know how fast they are — or do they just think the whole world is slow?

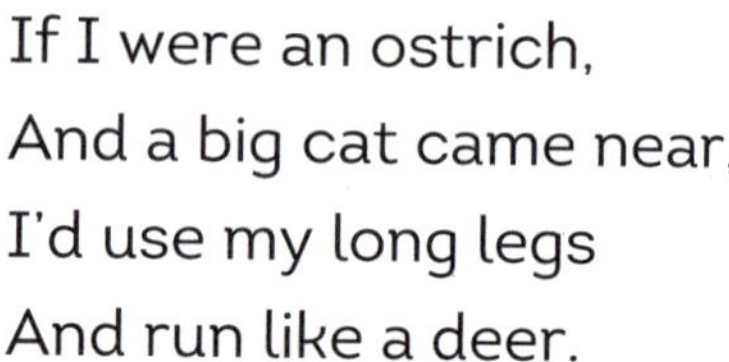

OSTRICH

by Darcy Day Zoells

If I were an ostrich,
I'd use my keen sight
To spot leopards and lions
Before they could bite.

If I were an ostrich,
And a big cat came near,
I'd use my long legs
And run like a deer.

If I were an ostrich,
All full of dread,
I'd never, ever, ever
Bury my head.

If I were an ostrich
They'd say, "You can't fly!"
But if I were an ostrich
I'd certainly try.

There are two ostrich species, and they are both native to Africa. Ostriches are the largest living bird in the world, weighing between 250 and 300 pounds and they can be up to 9 feet tall, They dig their nests in the ground and check on their eggs, but don't bury their heads in the sand.

Flightless Birds

penguin
kiwi
cassowary
kakapo
ostrich
dodo
Darwin's rhea
Fuegian steamer duck
flightless cormorant
Titicaca grebe

WONDERFUZZ

Do leopards and tigers need camouflage spots and stripes so they can be good hunters, or do they have them just for looks?

THIMBLETHOUGHT

Unlike most cats, leopards are good swimmers and are one of the few cats that like water — but they are not as comfortable in the water as tigers.

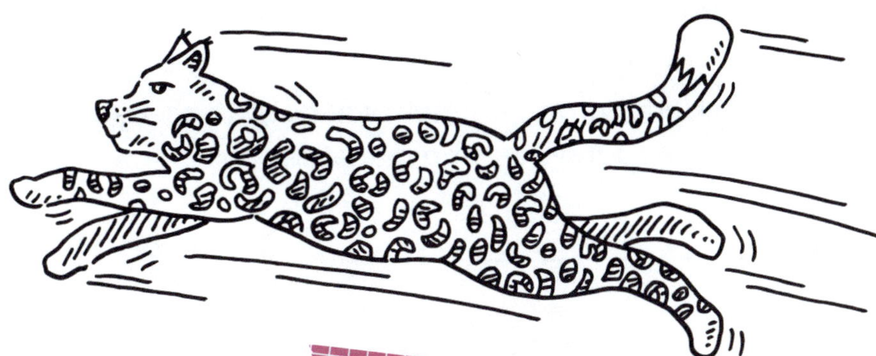

STUCK

by Cynthia Cotten

Is Leopard's stomach tied in knots
Because he cannot change his spots?
No stripes, no hearts, no polka dots,
No paisley, checks, or tartan plaid.
Leopard cannot change his spots.
I wonder if this makes him sad.

Elise's choice

Animals with Spots

leopard - cheetah - jaguar
hyena - dalmatian
spotted bush snake
Burmese python
leopard gecko
giraffe - fallow deer - axis deer
snowy owl - spotted sandpiper
tiger quoll
ladybug - spotted lanternfly

Most leopards are light in color and have dark spots on their fur. They are very solitary and leave urine, poop, and scratches on trees to warn other leopards to stay away. They can run very fast, leap, and climb trees. They spend most of their time camouflaged up in the branches.

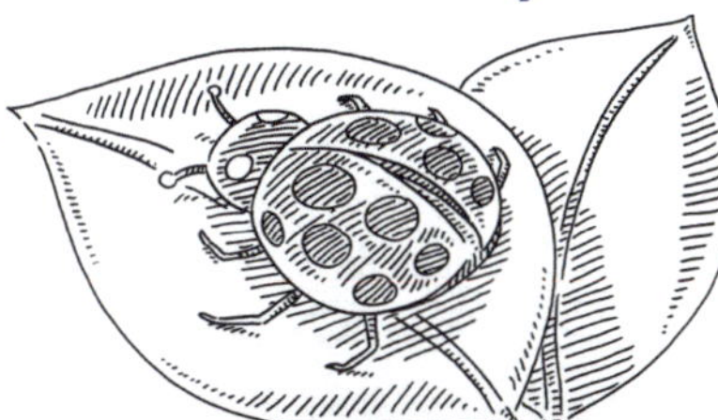

TOOT!

by Rochelle Melander

The rooting tooting manatee floated to the top.
Breathed and blew a bubble before she let it pop.
Hungry for her lunch, she cut the cheese and then
the rooting tooting manatee sank below again.

Jenny's choice

Note: Manatees are missing a swim bladder, the organ that helps fish adjust their buoyancy. No worries! Manatees hold in gas to float to the top and release it to sink down.

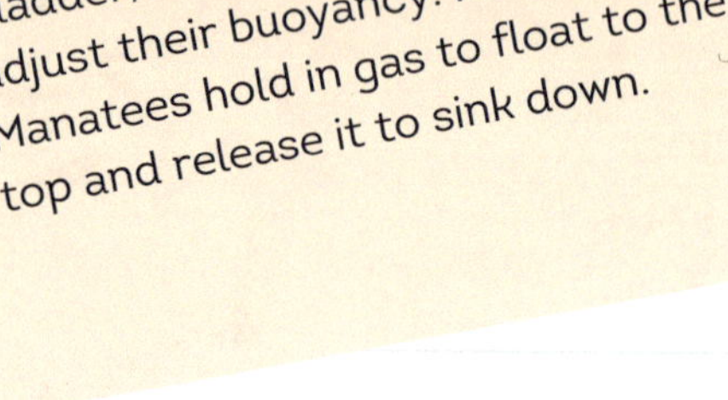

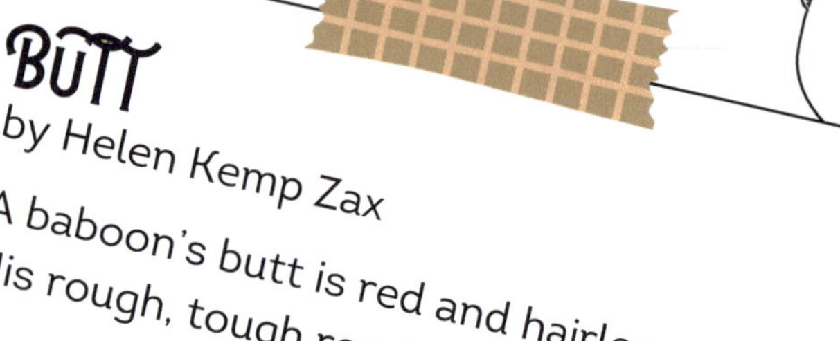

Sam's newest choice (Make up your mind, Sam, or we'll never be finished with our report!)

BUTT

by Helen Kemp Zax

A baboon's butt is red and hairless.
His rough, tough rear's for sitting – chairless.

WONDERFUZZ

How many times a day does the average person fart?

THIMBLETHOUGHT

Manatees live in water that is 60 degrees or warmer. They may look fat and insulated, but their bodies are mostly made up of their stomach and intestines.

WONDERFUZZ

Could penguin poop freeze immediately (after coming out of penguins' butts) and become POOPsicles?

THIMBLETHOUGHT

Penguins can shoot their poop out of their butts — up to four feet.

Amy's new choice.

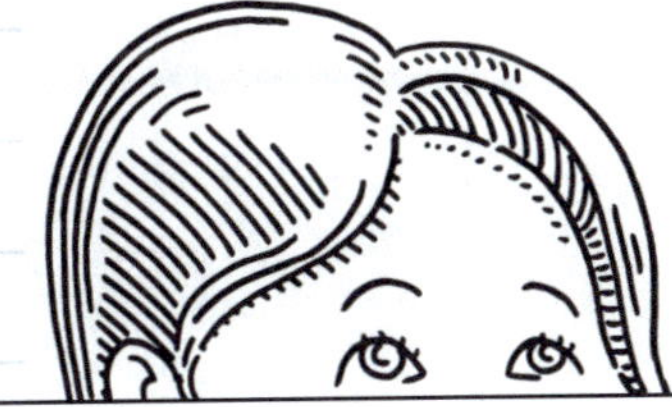

The colony at Port Lockroy is home to over 1,000 gentoo penguins. In fact, half the island is reserved for visiting tourists, while the other half is reserved entirely for the penguins living there.

Port Lockroy, Antarctica

by Sara Matson

If you visit Port Lockroy – it's near the south pole –
you might see some penguins out for a stroll,
slowly and aimlessly waddling around
or sunning their backs, stretched-out on the ground
or sitting or squawking or nesting or napping
or pecking or preening or fledging or flapping.
Hundreds of penguins means . . . well, can you guess?
That many birds on one island – BIG mess!
So go to Port Lockroy; you'll marvel and gawk.
But . . .
Beware of the guano and watch where you walk!

I want to do worms versus caterpillars as my new choice.

ONE-ON-ONE

by Robyn Hood Black

"I am Worm,"
said Worm.
"I have no feet.
"I am long and smooth.
"My name has one sound."

"Caterpillar!"
announced Caterpillar.
"Appendages galore.
"Spectacular segments, moving together.
"Melodious appellation!"

"Branches beckon," declared Caterpillar.
"Jubilant journeys!"

"I am off to the dirt," said Worm.
"Have a nice day."

Butterflies and moths start their lives as an egg, then a larva, and then a caterpillar. Then they eat constantly, outgrow and shed their skin, and latch onto a branch to form a cocoon. After metamorphosis occurs, they emerge as butterflies and moths.

WONDERFUZZ

I wonder if butterflies keep any of their old caterpillar memories?

THIMBLETHOUGHT

Caterpillars increase their body size by as much as 1000 times.

Fun Facts about Worms

Worms have been around longer than dinosaurs.

Worms have five hearts and are cold-blooded.

Worms have no arms, legs, eyes, or teeth.

Worms build tunnels in the soil that help plants grow.

In one acre of land, there can be more than a million earthworms.

WRIGGLE AWAY

By Kristy Dempsey

The earthworm's not an inchworm.
He's longer than you thinkth.
Though it isn't quite a cinch
to determine his true length.

He squinches and he flinches.
He's not so very firm-y.
If you place him on a ruler,
he'll continue being squirmy.

I think the reason why the worm
won't let the measure take
is if you see how long he is,
you'll fear he is a snake.

There are thousands of different species of earthworms around the world. They have no eyes, but are light-sensitive and become paralyzed if exposed to light too long.

THIMBLETHOUGHT

Earthworms have no hearts, but they have five pairs of aortic arches that carry blood forward to the front and backward to the rear.

WONDERFUZZ

Since they have no hearts, can earthworms feel love?

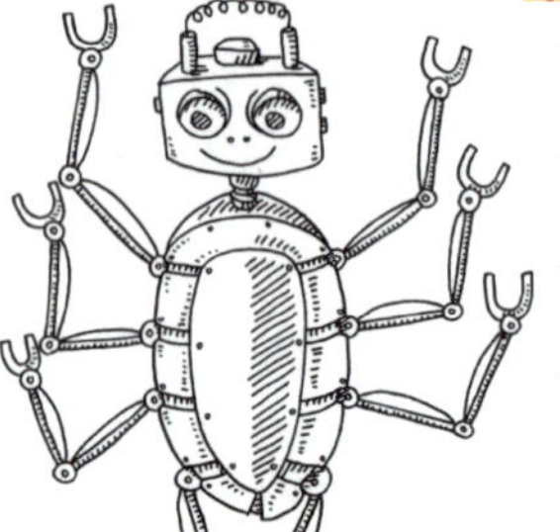

Cicadas

by Marcie Flinchum Atkins

Cicada Chorus at Dawn
ZZZZZZTTTTT-ZZZZZZTTTTT!

Cicada Bumbles Through the Air
THUMP!

Discarded Exoskeletons Line the Driveway
CRUNCH!

Mrs. Booker asks, "Did anyone choose cicadas? There were SO MANY cicadas this year — enough for each of you to have one million of them!"

Onomatopoeia = words that capture sounds like: ZZZZZZTTTTT-ZZZZZZTTTTT! THUMP! CRUNCH!

Note: In 2024, two different broods of cicadas, totaling more than a trillion, emerged at the same time in the United States. These same two broods will not emerge together again for another 221 years!

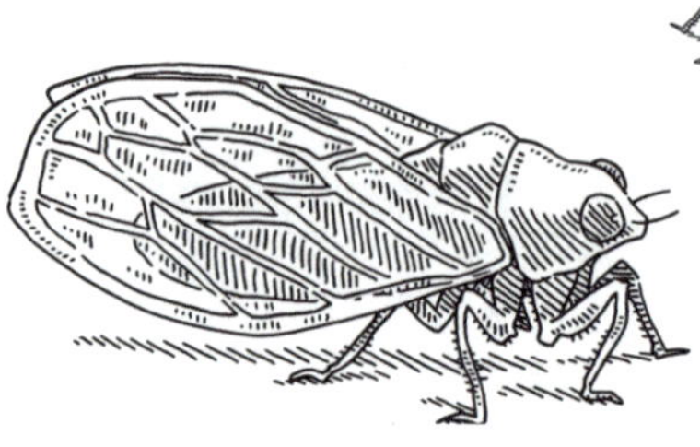

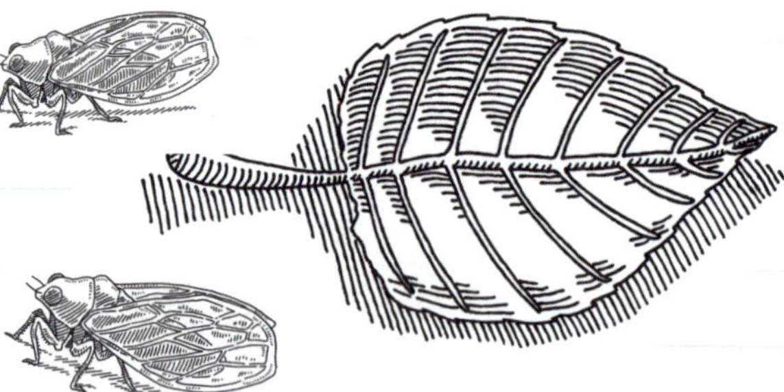

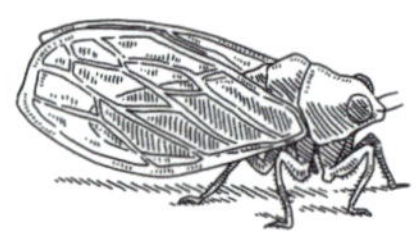

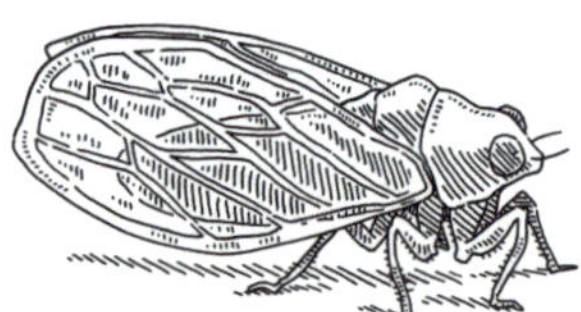

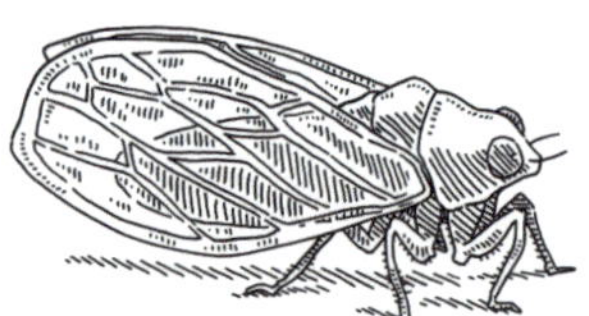

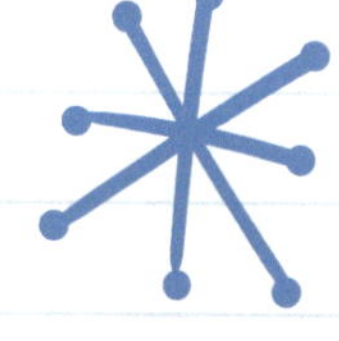

WONDERFUZZ

Do cicadas get tired of staying underground for so long?

THIMBLETHOUGHT

Cicadas have one of the longest lifespans of any insect, 13-17 years, but only a fraction of that time is above ground. The rest is spent underground feeding on liquid from plant roots.

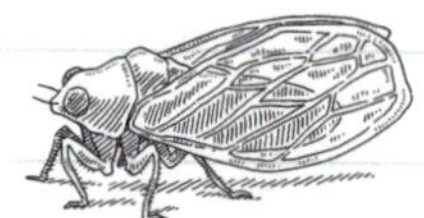

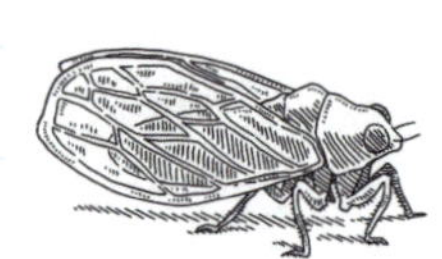

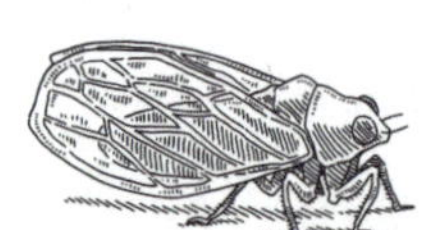

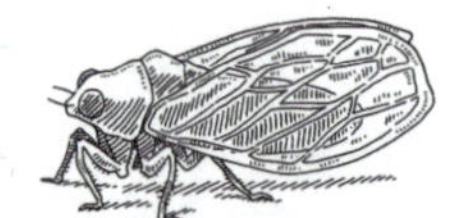

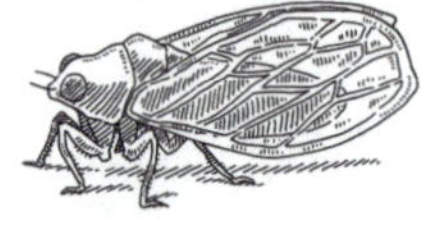

Axolotl

by Marcie Flinchum Atkins

Along the murky lakebed floor
scoots a walking carnivore.

His tail propels him through the night –
a tale of eating by moon's light.

His four short legs swish and swim
until a foe chomps on a limb.

But do not worry: for his arm,
he regrows what has been harmed.

His frilly head is graced with gills
and underwater breathing skills.

His suction-powered mouth devours.
It's one of many superpowers.

My newest choice!

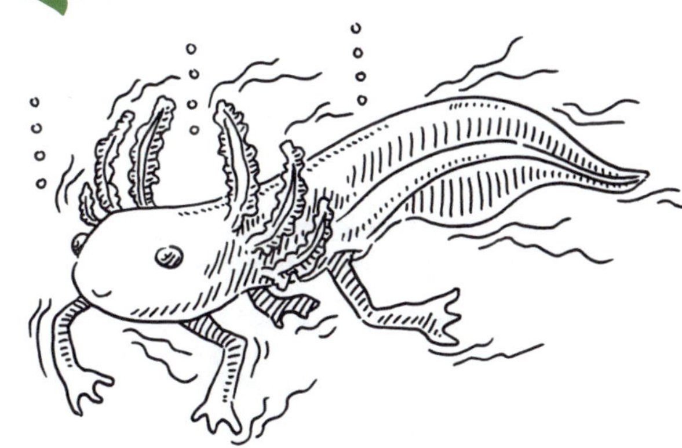

ELISE IS A CICADA-HEAD

by Clara

Elise says,
"You should choose cicadas."
I strongly DISagree.
She mistakenly thinks
she's our supervisor, but
she's not the boss of me!

A **stanza** is a group of lines in a poem.
A **couplet** is a two-line stanza.

WONDERFUZZ

How is it that thousands of honeybees are able to cooperate in a beehive — when just 8 of us are struggling to work together?

THIMBLETHOUGHT

Scientists around the world are studying how axolotls can regenerate missing eyes, limbs, and even parts of their brains. Amazing!

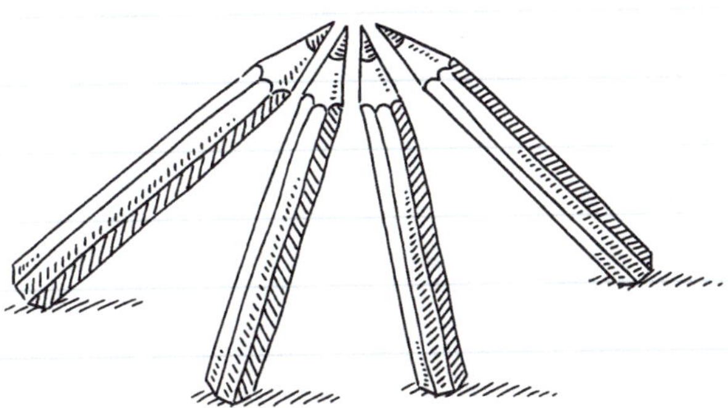

TEAMWORK GONE BERSERK

by Clara

We always disagree.
We're failing as a team.
But our teacher says no. No,
we can't change midstream.
She says, "Just remember:
you're fair and faithful friends.
Forget this angry nonsense.
It's time to make amends!"

"CICADA-HEAD?! REALLY?!!!"
by Clara

Elise cannot believe
I called her a
CICADA-HEAD.

She was "attacked" in the face
by cicadas last summer,
so the topic fills her with dread.

I said "I'm sorry if I hurt your feelings."
She shouted, "IF? IF!!!"
She is still so, so mad.

And I am
so, so, so, so, so,
so sad.

WONDERFUZZ
Are there any animals who feel strong emotions like humans?

THIMBLETHOUGHT
Hachiko was a Japanese dog who went to the train station daily for almost 10 years to wait for his owner (who had died). Some people think Hachiko was not just loyal, but had strong feelings of sadness, love, and hope.

Ways to Say "I'm Sorry"

I messed up.
My bad.
I didn't mean to do that.
I owe you an apology.
Can you forgive me?
How can I make things right?
I feel so wrong about this.
I'm ashamed.
I wish I hadn't done that.
Hey, let's go play pickleball!

The Art of Apologizing After Hurting a Friend

by Eileen Spinelli

You can say it: "I'm sorry."
You can hand-craft a card.
You can write it in verse.
It's not really that hard.
You can buy a small gift
at a favorite store.
You can pick a bouquet,
lay it at the front door.
You can sing it. Or paint it.
Or bake it.
And then –
try never to hurt
that person again.

WONDERFUZZ
Are there any friendships where NO ONE needed to apologize for something?

I'm sorry!

I APOLOGIZE.

Lo siento

Here's a little note I wrote. It's not very long, but I think it says enough.

Dear Elise,

I know you feel quite a bit of hate.
I tried to bite my tongue — too late.
I made you mad, but can we quit
this war we're in? I'm sorry.

Love,
Clara

Dear Clara,
I forgive you. Just NEVER EVER call me a cicada-head again!!!

Here's the note that Elise gave to me

THIMBLETHOUGHT
Apologizing is not just good manners or an expression of empathy, it is an important part of healing a relationship.

WEEKEND GETAWAY

EXERCISE #17: SOCIAL STUDIES CONNECTIONS
Write about something you've learned about in social studies (geography, history, etc.) this year.

Bound is a contronym (a word with two opposite meanings).

Meaning #1:
tied, secured, not going anywhere.

Meaning #2:
going somewhere.

BOUND

by Marilyn Garcia

Clara stuffed her suitcase for the family summer trip
(toothbrush, swim fins, teddy bear
bucket, shovel, underwear) –
then bound her suitcase tightly down
so it would never slip.

Clara, Brother, Father, Mother climbed into their car
(clicket-clack, buckle snap
ready in the front and back).
Now they're bound for summer fun –
adventures near and far!

I know that this poem is about a DIFFERENT Clara, but it could be about ME and MY family! I love-love-love reading poems with MY name in them. CLARA, JAMES, and VERA are my favorite names EVER!!!

THIMBLE THOUGHT
A favorite vacation destination in the U.S. is a National Park — and there are 63 to choose from!

WONDERFUZZ
When birds fly south for the winter, do they feel like they're going on vacation?

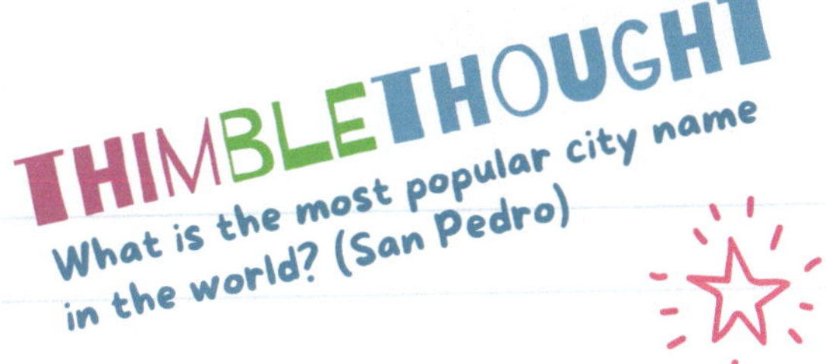

THIMBLETHOUGHT

What is the most popular city name in the world? (San Pedro)

Vacation Question

by Calef Brown

Dear Diary,
Here's an inquiry,
that I think, for me,
requires a degree
of mulling over:

Was I in Dover,
or was I in Kent?
I just can't remember
to which one I went.
A park, I recall,
and a cottage for rent.
Or did I go camping
and sleep in a tent?
I guess I'll just wait
for the postcard I sent,
to fondly remind me
how time there was spent.

An **epistolary poem** looks and sounds like a letter written to a friend or other reader.

Some "Twin" Towns

Paris, France
Paris, Texas

Manila, Philippines
Manila, Arkansas

Athens, Greece
Athens, Georgia

Memphis, Egypt
Memphis, Tennessee

Kent, England
Kent, Washington

WONDERFUZZ

How do sea turtles remember where they were born — thousands of miles away?

EXERCISE #18: JOBS IN OUR COMMUNITY
Write about the jobs that some of the people you know have.

It's Assembly Day!

HELP WANTED?

by Eric E. Peterson

Finding a job is no easy task.
Where do I look, and whom do I ask?

Can I make pizza? I don't really know,
And even if hired, can I make any dough?

Not sure if I nailed my last interview,
Working alongside a house building crew.

A doctor could take a long time in school,
If I had the patients, that could be cool.

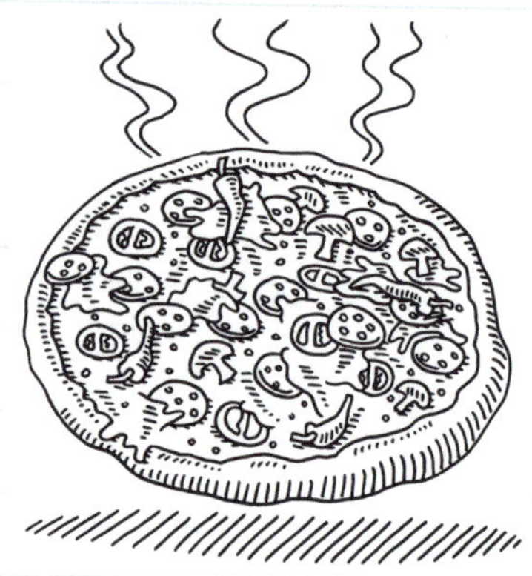

THIMBLE THOUGHT
One of the most universally embarrassing moments is to wave at someone who is not waving at YOU.

Uncle Frank is Zooming in
for our Career Day assembly.
He will talk about being
a professional artist.
Mrs. Booker picked me
to introduce him
and on the way up to the stage
I tripped
and almost fell on my face!
EMBARRASSING!!!

How many different jobs do most people have (during their whole lifetime)?

Common Kinds of Artists

illustrators - painters
photographers - filmmakers
digital artists - graphic designers
sculptors - printmakers
weavers - quilters - knitters
silkscreen artists - tattoo artists
fashion designers
interior designers - architects
actors - comedians
dancers - performance artists
singers - musicians
writers - poets - screenwriters
chefs - food artists

WONDERFUZZ

What is the most famous piece of art?

THE ARTIST

by Molly Lorenz

If a parrot prints a pattern
from a pink and purple palette
or a penguin paints a portrait
of a playful perky pet . . .

If a donkey draws a donut
with a dozen dabs and dots
or a dingo doodles drawings
dressed in dungarees with spots . . .

If a weasel weaves a basket
with weeping willow reed
or a woodchuck whittles wood
from windswept tumbleweed . . .

If a cat creates a castle
from a chunk or clump of clay
or chooses colored paper
to cut and clip away . . .

If a badger builds a background
using brushes that are new
or blows glass beads for bracelets
in hues of brown and blue . . .

Then you can be an artist too!

THIMBLETHOUGHT

Between 1912 and 1948, the Olympics included ART and medals were given for masterpieces of painting, sculpture, music, literature, and architecture that were inspired by sports.

THIMBLETHOUGHT

Almost 2 million men in the U.S. are stay-at-home dads who are the daily, primary caregivers for their children (18 and under).

Career Day

by Eric E. Peterson

It's career day in my fourth-grade class.
I think my dad will probably pass.
You see, he stays at home to care
For our family when we're there.

The CEO of house and home,
The taxi driver when we roam.
Gardener when the grass is tall,
The EMT for when we fall.

On the weekend, you know who
Will be cooking BBQ.
He likes to watch the NFL
And nurse us when we don't feel well.

Fact is he does this all for free.
He truly is our VIP.

Each of these words is a type of abbreviation called an **initialism.** With initialisms, we say each letter **(V-I-P).**

CEO = Chief Executive Officer
EMT = Emergency Medical Technician
BBQ = barbeque
NFL = National Football League
VIP = Very Important Person

WONDERFUZZ

What kinds of small jobs (for family and neighbors) can kids do besides walking a dog or pulling weeds?

THIMBLETHOUGHT

Women who work full-time, year-round jobs earn 84 cents for every dollar men earn, and women who work part-time make even less.

WONDERFUZZ

How many people decide on a career when they're a kid and actually end up doing it as a grown-up?

Job Juggler

by Padma Venkatraman

There's that juggler. Look at her go!
She doesn't juggle balls. No, no.

By day, she studies oceanography,
sometimes in a landlocked laboratory,
sometimes on a ship at sea.
At her desk, she writes and writes,
stories and poems every night.

Think she has two jobs? Well, actually,
she has got at least three!

Scientist, writer, and guess what other?
She also loves being a mother!

Outstanding Women Scientists

Rosalind Franklin discovered the structure of DNA.
Caroline Herschel discovered eight comets.
Marie Curie discovered radioactive elements.
Jane Goodall realized chimpanzees do human actions.
Dorothy Hodgkin helped to develop insulin, penicillin, and vitamin B-12.

EXERCISE #19: DREAM JOBS

What are some jobs that you might like? Be daring! Be creative! Think BIG!

ESPIONAGE

by J. David Martinez

Espionage is
French for "spying
pigeon." Honest!*
Next time you see one
eating a *French* fry
remember:
pigeon spy!
And watch your back
as you walk by
especially if
it's missing an eye
and
wearing a tie –
that's how you know
it's a
pigeon spy!

WONDERFUZZ

What is the best way to become a professional actor?

What would be the BEST job ever?
Jade says an astronaut.
Elise says an actor. James says a spy.
How about being an actor
who plays a spy-der!!

Jade gave me her Space Center ticket stub! After she becomes an astronaut, this will be worth a LOT but I will never sell it!!

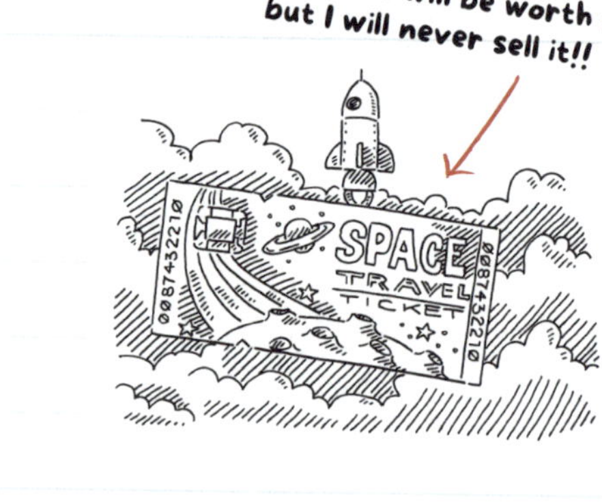

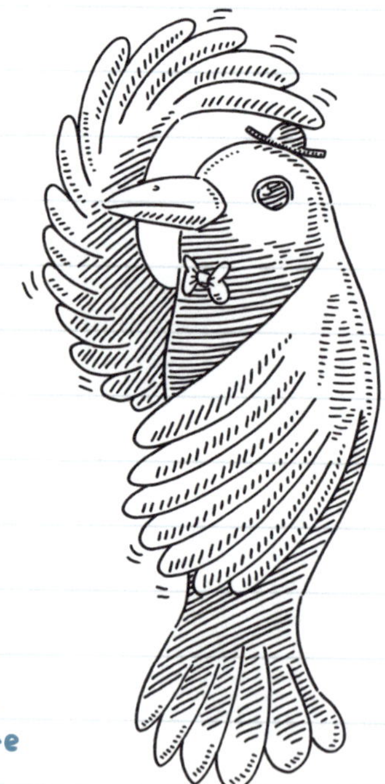

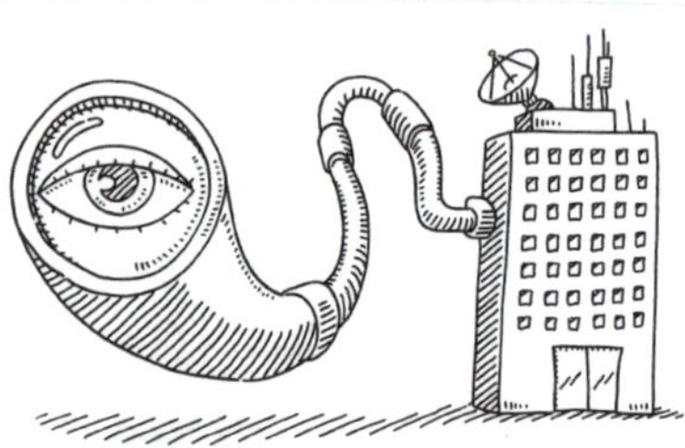

THIMBLETHOUGHT

Before there were drones, there were pigeons that flew ahead to gather information — for ancient Roman armies, for German soldiers in WWI, and with cameras attached to them across Cuba for the CIA.

*Not honest. "Espionage" just means "spying," not "spying pigeon." But pigeons and spying do have a long history . . . Look it up!

WONDERFUZZ

Are tarantulas dangerous — or misunderstood?

THIMBLETHOUGHT

Several hundred years ago a "dancing epidemic" was linked to a spider bite. It started in Taranto, Italy, which gave the name "tarantula" to the spider and the name "tarantella" to the dance.

TARANTULA

by Patricia J. Franz

Dear Talent Agent,

I am typecast all the time
(Trick-or-Treat décor and fangs).
Makes me touchy, a bit timid,
though I have tremendous talent.
I can tango, tap, and twist. I can tarantella.
Ballet is more my style.
I've trained since I was two.

My titular talent:
I tip-toe at twilight.
But audiences tremble
at my twisted, tickly torso.
It's tricky I know,
troubling, and so
take your time. Let me know?
I'd love to try out for the troupe.

Signed,
Tarantula in a Tutu

A **mask poem** is from the point of view of something that doesn't usually talk – often an animal.

Simile is an explicit comparison between two things or ideas, usually using "as" or "like."

James is like a rocket,
ready to launch.
He ignites easily —
just get him excited
by talking about
dogs or tattoos
or video games —
and he's ready for liftoff!

by Janet Wong

We all know how we should sit.
And, YES, we can do it!

Criss-cross, on our seat.
Quiet voices, quiet feet.

Eyes up front. Hands in lap.
Listen, laugh, and clap, clap, clap!

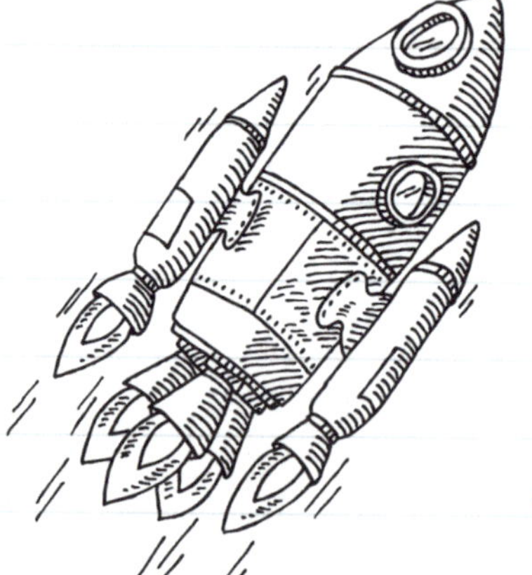

WONDERFUZZ

What's the difference between someone with "an active mind" and someone with "ADHD"?

THIMBLETHOUGHT

Many scientists, writers, and artists with ADHD have very successful careers, in large part because of their ability to focus on what they're doing for hours on end, called hyperfocus.

PLAYING ATTENTION

by Allan Wolf

Our teacher said to pay attention.
But I thought she said play attention.
That's why I'm sitting in Detention.

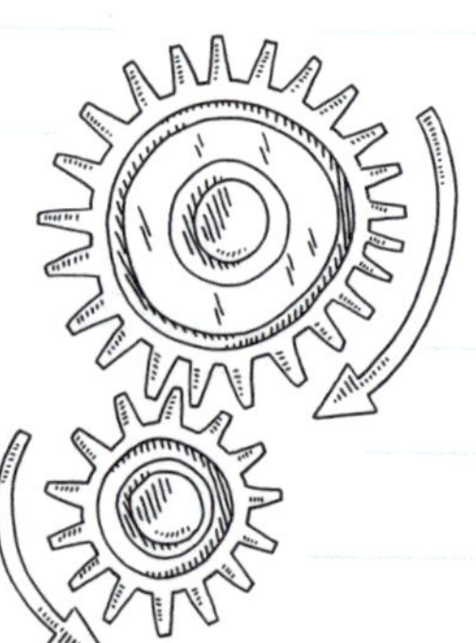

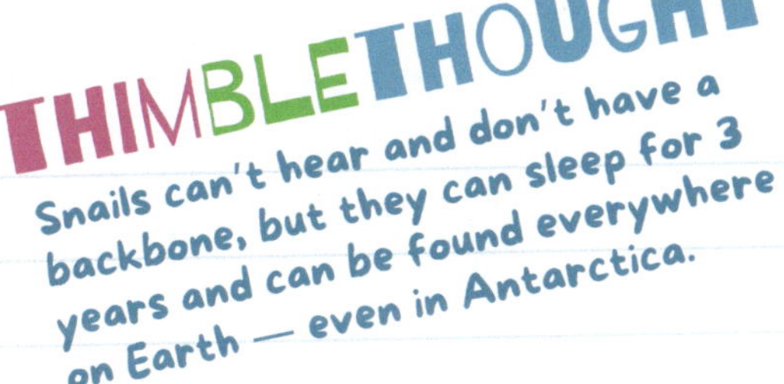

A **lyrical poem** expresses the poet's emotions – often in first-person (with *I*).

WONDERFUZZ

People can pay attention to more than one thing at a time, right?

PLEASE PAY ATTENTION

by Elizabeth Steinglass

Away in the distance
a grown-up is talking.

The mic sounds like ducklings
squeaking and squawking.

Away in the distance
there's a slide of a snail.

I wonder how far
it can glide on its trail.

Bernardo is rocking.
There's wind in the trees.

I think I can hear them
unfurling their leaves.

Does a snail ever wish
it could knit a soft suit,

or hop on one foot
and not have to scoot?

They have thousands of teeth –
imagine their braces!

Hey, I've tied thirteen knots
in Marie's sneaker laces!

Ms. Bellingham taps me.
What she says really stings –

when I'm paying attention
to so many things!

Weakened Before the Weekend
by Your Tired Teacher

It's the end of the week.
I'm so tired, I can't speak.
My mind and physique
are WEAKENED.

But tomorrow: the mall!
And I'll play pickleball,
steep, and goof off
all WEEKEND!

Mrs. Booker has a little poem she wants to share with us . . .

THIMBLE THOUGHT

Benjamin Banneker created the first clock made entirely out of wooden pieces (which he hand-carved). It was incredibly precise and worked for decades afterwards!

WONDERFUZZ

Are there places where people only have to work 3 or 4 days/week?

Tick Tock

by Dolores Andral

Because I watched the clock,
it stopped.
It didn't tick.
It didn't tock.
On a Friday afternoon,
the weekend near and coming soon.
I gave the clock an icy glare,
the time not going anywhere.
I huffed and puffed and made a face.
Frozen time trapped in the case.
Hopping mad, I said, "Let's dance!"
Only then did hands advance.
I did The Twist,
The clock: The Spin.
We hokey pokey'd,
hands all in.
Because I danced around the clock.
It ticked.
It tocked.
It rocked.

EXERCISE #20: ON YOUR OWN
Write about something happening in your life outside of school.

Amy's birthday is tomorrow at noon
(mine is a long time away; it's in June).

Tonight we went over to help them bake
cookies and cupcakes and birthday cake.

Tomorrow we'll stay all day and all night
for a sleepover with a pillow fight!

I love parties. Give me ALL the treats:
I'll eat EVERYTHING, savory and sweet!

RSVP

by Joyce Uglow

Répondez S'il Vous Plaît –
I really need to know today.

It's a party at the lake.
There will be birthday cake!

Are you coming? Yes or no?
Count you in? I sure hope so!

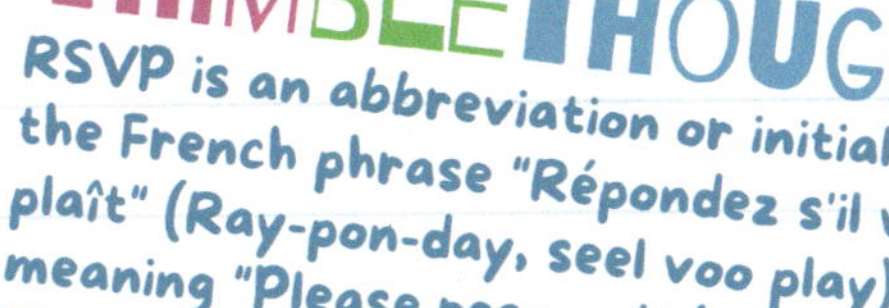

THIMBLETHOUGHT
RSVP is an abbreviation or initialism of the French phrase "Répondez s'il vous plaît" (Ray-pon-day, seel voo play) meaning "Please respond" (or literally "Respond, if it pleases you"), which asks you to let your host know if you can come or not.

WONDERFUZZ
Do wild animals celebrate birthdays?

THIMBLETHOUGHT

How did candy get its name? Probably from the Arabic qandi, Persian qand, or Sanskrit khanda — which are all words for "sugar."

WHO 8 THE CANDY?

by Linda Picaro Tarantino

1, 2, 3, 4
Candy, Candy, I want more
5, 6, 7, "8"
That's what I did - I couldn't wait

Candy is delicious
So much sweetness in it
I just have to eat some
Right this very minute

Candy is delicious
And so very yummy
Quick, quick, I just want some
In my hungry tummy

1, 2, 3, 4
Candy, candy, I DID eat more
5, 6, 7, "8"
That's what I did - I couldn't wait

Most Popular Candy in the U.S.

Reese's Peanut Butter Cups
M&M's
Hot Tamales
Skittles
Sour Patch Kids
Starburst
Hershey's Kisses
Snickers
KitKat
3 Musketeers
Butterfinger
Crunch Bars

WONDERFUZZ

What are the MOST popular healthy-for-you sweet treats?

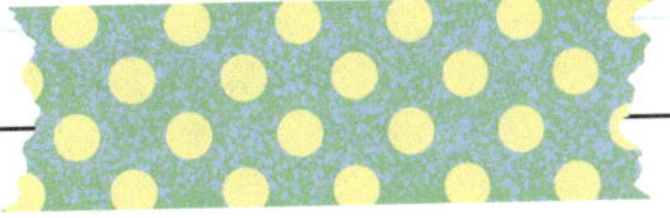

Would You Like To Bake?

by Carol Varsalona

You can beat two eggs
Around and around
While the beat makes
A loud wheezing sound.
You can combine and whip
The delicious dough,
But not too fast –
It could fly and flow!
Before you bake, pause.
Here's some last-minute advice:
Add a half a cup of nuts
And a dash of spice!

THIMBLETHOUGHT

Chocolate chip cookies were made by mistake by a baker who put bits of broken chocolate into the batter thinking the chocolate would melt — but it didn't. Then chocolate CHIPS were created because this cookie was such a hit!

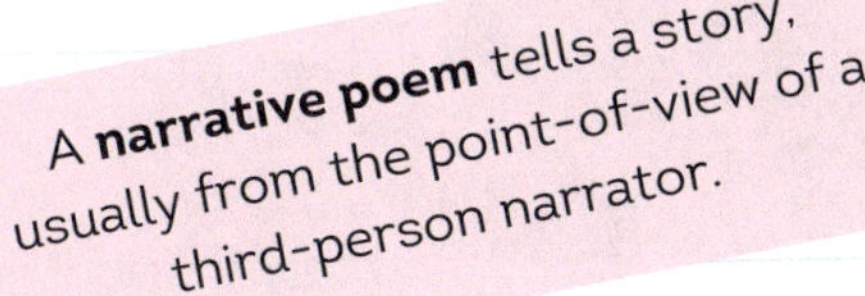

A **narrative poem** tells a story, usually from the point-of-view of a third-person narrator.

Cupcakes

by Lyn Jekowsky

Jenny Giraffe
complained of a neck ache
because she just baked
about ten thousand cupcakes.

She was planning a party
for Elephant's birthday.
All grassland's wildlife
were welcome the next day!

WONDERFUZZ

Is it true that herbs and spices were as valuable as gold in the Middle Ages?

THIMBLETHOUGHT

Thomas Jefferson is said to have brought a waffle iron home to the U.S. from France around 1789, starting the trend of having waffle parties.

WAFFLES

by Leslie Degnan

I feel a bit under the weather.
Tissues pile up to the sky.
I'm running a fever, I'm chilled to the bone,
And a frog in my throat just dropped by.

I feel a bit under the weather.
Mom says, "You look fine to me."
I can't eat a thing, I'm as sick as a dog,
And as pale as a ghost. Can't you see?

"I see that you're under the weather.
Waffles won't help much, of course."
Waffles today? Is it Saturday?
I'm so hungry I could eat a horse!

Fun Waffle Facts

1. The soles of Nike's first pair of sneakers were made using a real waffle iron.
2. The world's biggest waffle was 8 feet long and weighed 110 pounds.
3. The Waffle House sells 145 waffles a minute.
4. EGGO waffles were originally called Froffles (frozen + waffles).

So many **idioms** or expressions here:
under the weather (sick),
pile up to the sky (pile high);
running a fever (having a fever);
chilled to the bone (very cold);
frog in my throat (sick);
sick as a dog (very sick);
pale as a ghost (very pale);
so hungry I could eat a horse (very hungry).

WONDERFUZZ

Why do people say, "Feed a cold, starve a fever?"

TAKE IT EASY
by Clara

First stop for our all-day party:
the local carnival.
We ride the giant spinning thing,
then the ferris wheel,
and finally the roller coaster.
I'm feeling queasy.
My tummy is saying,
"Hey, take it easy!"

WONDER FUZZ
What's the best way to become braver?

THIMBLETHOUGHT
Roller coasters are called that because a chain helps the car ROLL up to the top of a hill, but then it is released and the car can COAST down.

ROLLER COASTER
by Megan Litwin

Big, fast, twirly.
Bigger, faster, twirlier!
Biggest, fastest, twirliest!!

Guess which one
made my stomach
the swirliest?

Comparatives compare 2 things and **superlatives** compare 3 or more: big, *bigger*, ***biggest***; fast, *faster*, ***fastest;*** twirly, *twirlier*, ***twirliest.***

JUMP!
by Leslie Degnan

Is it that you can't,
Or is it that you won't?

I'm certain you can do it,
I believe in you. You don't?

You're almost to the top.
Don't look down! You shouldn't.

Shuffle to the end and . . . JUMP!
I didn't think you couldn't!

BIRTHDAY SPLASH

by Lisa Billa

My birthday party's in full swing, here in our backyard;
the bounce house is a pirate ship – this long balloon, a sword!

The outbursts from our battle – though it's all in fun –
fill the air with joyful noise as the deck is overrun.

The piñata's stuffed with bubblegum and lollipops and stuff;
this bat will break it open, if I hit it hard enough.

But when I take the blindfold off, the view is not so grand.
Dark clouds announce a thunderstorm – this might not go as planned.

I'm sure I feel a raindrop, then right away, one more –
now, a nearby lightning crash, and bigger drops galore!

Mom looks slightly worried; Dad just shakes his head . . .
it's much too wet for outdoor games – we'll play inside instead!

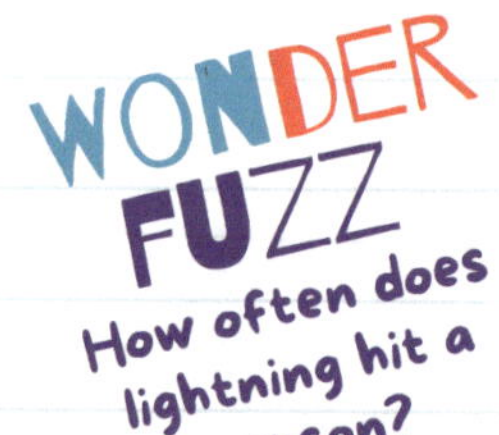

THIMBLETHOUGHT

A thunderstorm is a rain shower that contains lightning. Scientists estimate that there are nearly 2000 thunderstorms in progress around the world at any moment.

RAIN
by Vicki Wilke

It's really raining cats and dogs,
said Grammy to my Paw.
I couldn't wait to look outside –
but this is what I saw.

No wagging tails, or soggy fur,
and nothing to explain.
Just lots and lots
and lots and lots
and lots and lots
of RAIN!

THIMBLETHOUGHT

Synonyms for rain include: sprinkle, drizzle, mizzle, Scotch mist, precipitation, deluge, cloudburst, torrent, pikels, and frog-strangler.

Party + Weather + Bad Luck = Rainout

Birds can fly away
and hide from this cold cloudburst —
trees sit shivering

A **haiku** is an ancient Japanese poem form that usually consists of three lines with syllable counts of 5-7-5

PET
by Laura Renauld

It's raining cats and dogs, you say?
I knew a pup would come my way!
I race outside to claim my pet,
But all I get is soaking wet.

Only 3 of us friends can stay for dinner and the sleepover. Amy's parents are taking us to a FANCY restaurant downtown!

How To Eat At A Swanky Restaurant With Your Friend's Family (If You Never Want To Be Invited Again)*

by Joan Riordan

Chomp
Gnaw
Slurp

Smack
Spit
Burp

*as learned from personal experience

WONDERFUZZ

How are you supposed to behave at a fancy restaurant?

THIMBLETHOUGHT

Slurping food is considered poor manners in Western culture, but slurping your noodles in Asian culture is considered an appreciation for your meal.

WONDERFUZZ

Is it true that Queen Elizabeth II ate bananas with a knife and fork?

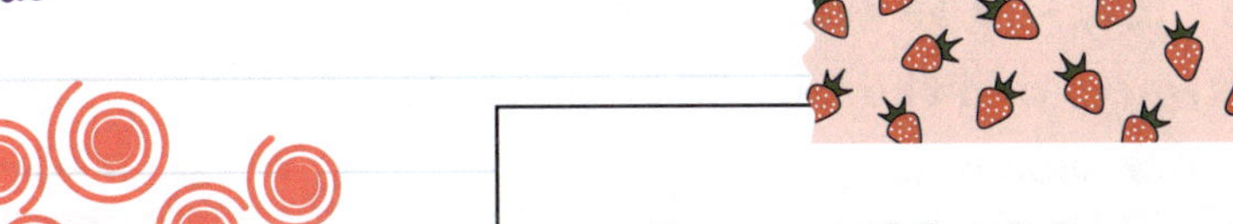

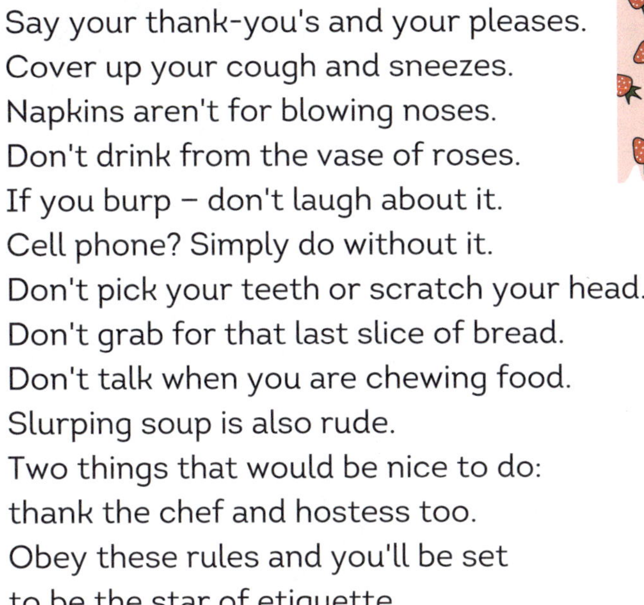

Table Manners 101

by Eileen Spinelli

Say your thank-you's and your pleases.
Cover up your cough and sneezes.
Napkins aren't for blowing noses.
Don't drink from the vase of roses.
If you burp – don't laugh about it.
Cell phone? Simply do without it.
Don't pick your teeth or scratch your head.
Don't grab for that last slice of bread.
Don't talk when you are chewing food.
Slurping soup is also rude.
Two things that would be nice to do:
thank the chef and hostess too.
Obey these rules and you'll be set
to be the star of etiquette.

Basic Manners

1. Be kind
2. Wait your turn
3. Don't tease
4. Use a napkin
5. Introduce yourself
6. Say "excuse me"
7. Say "please" and "thank you"
8. Express gratitude
9. Knock when a door is closed
10. Send "thank you" cards

Thank you!

THIMBLETHOUGHT

The number one rule of etiquette is the "Golden Rule": Treat other people like you want them to treat you.

FOUR KIDS ON A PATIO

by Clara

Four kids on a patio are listening to scary stories
when they get to the swamp and the smallest one shrieks.
They point fingers at each other.
Coughing and choking, suddenly no one can speak . . .

Listening to Elise tell stories is like going to a scary movie. Here's my ticket stub from the last movie we saw together.

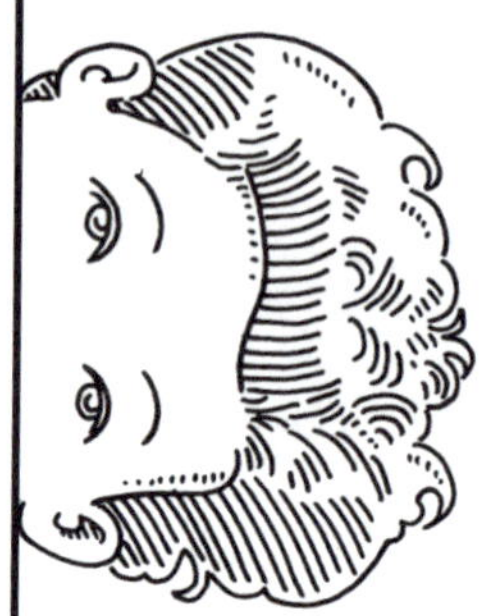

STINK!

by Pamela Taylor

I'm glad I have this time to think.
What is that smell? What is that stink?

Is it me or is it you?
I can't tell if it's us two.

Is it you? Is it your feet?
It can't be me – my feet smell sweet.

But wait! What's that? A cat that's black.
Are those white stripes on its back?

It's not you; it's not me –
Get up! Let's run! It's time to flee!

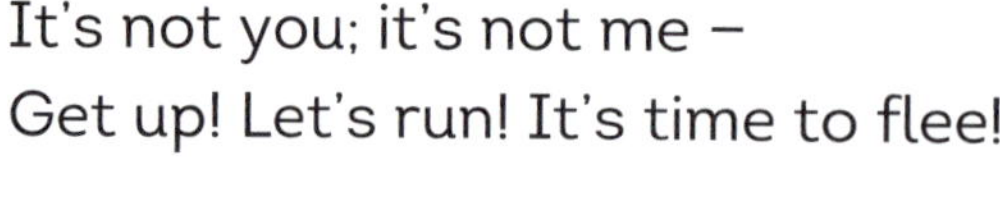

THIMBLETHOUGHT

A skunk will sometimes try to scare off predators with a warning dance or handstand to intimidate them.

WONDERFUZZ

Why do some people like to eat stinky things like blue cheese?

THIMBLETHOUGHT

Your feet have about 250,000 sweat glands and when your feet sweat, bacteria eats the sweat and gives off a smell like vinegar. Yuck!

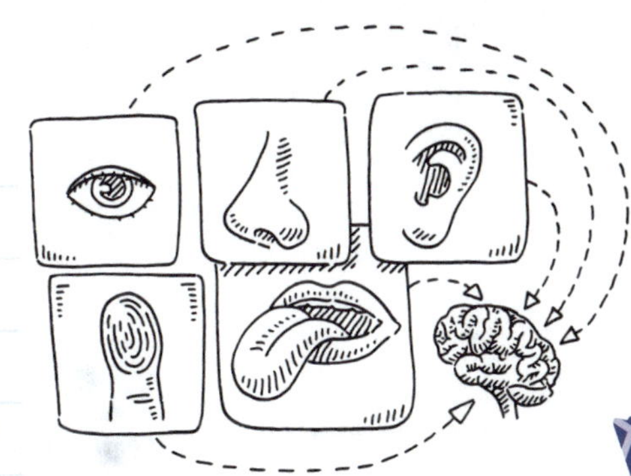

YOUR WOES
by Clara's Toes

If you didn't whine,
we'd be fine.
Your woes
involve
your nose,
not ours.
In fact,
we think we smell
like flowers!

TOES
by Kristy Dempsey

Toes are funny
Toes are sweet
Toes hang off the end of feet

Toes on babies
Toes down south
Toes inside a little mouth

Toes on grandpas
Toes with knots
Toes that look like tater tots

Lots of toes
Around the world
Fat and skinny, straight and curled

The only toes
That make me shrink
Are toes that fill my nose with stink

How to Prevent Smelly Feet

1. Wash your feet every day with soap.
2. Keep toenails short and clean.
3. Use foot powder.
4. Wear natural fiber (cotton, wool) socks.
5. Let shoes air out after wearing them.

A **stanza** is a group of lines in a poem. A **tercet** is a three-line stanza.

WONDERFUZZ

Does nature make certain things stinky so we'll be warned to stay away from them?

Slumber Party To-Do List

by Janet Wong

1. Tell some stories (not TOO scary)
2. Ignore the siblings' commentary
3. Watch a movie, play a game
4. Come up with a rock-star name
5. Eat some candy, eat more cake
6. Pinch your cheeks to stay awake
7. Invent a bouncy bullfrog dance
8. Don't split your pajama pants!
9. Have a fluffy pillow fight
10. Fall asleep around midnight

WONDERFUZZ

Why do most people wear special clothes (pajamas, nightgowns) when they sleep?

THIMBLETHOUGHT

Slumber parties and sleepovers are actually not really for slumbering or sleeping and usually result in sleep deprivation, but are still lots of fun!

THIMBLE THOUGHT

A whopper is also a tall tale, a lie, an untruth, a taradiddle, a humbug, an obliquity, and an exaggeration.

CLARA'S BFF

by Charles Ghigna

Who's my very bestest friend? I'd have to say Elise is.
Whenever we're together, the fun just never ceases.

She likes to make up stories and poems that are creepy.
She tells them during sleepovers just when we're getting sleepy.

Last night she told me one about a dinosaur outside.
She said she saw it coming here and we should run and hide.

She said it was all brown and gray and green and blue and red
With fire shooting out its mouth and horns upon its head.

It was taller than a building and bigger than a bus.
Elise said it was angry – and coming after us!

I ran and dove beneath the bed.
I closed my eyes and hid my head.

I couldn't sleep until she said that it was just a story.
She made it up tonight because she didn't want to bore me.

She said she'd tell another one, a happily ever after.
She saw me underneath the bed. We both broke out in laughter!

My bestie is Elise, and she can really tell a whopper.
Even though she scares me, I know I'll never stop her!

WONDERFUZZ

Why do so many people LOVE scary movies and stories?

Thanks (NOT) to Elise, I might have a nightmare now . . .
EXCEPT I brought my yeti to keep me safe.

Have You Ever Met a Yeti?

by Abby Oqueli

Have you ever met a yeti?
My mom gave one to me.
It's the fluffiest, cuddliest monster
That you will ever meet!

My brother has his own and
My sister has one too.
They live beneath our beds
And make sweet dreams come true.

If you suffer from the creepy-crawlies
That lurk within the dark of night
Get yourself a yeti
And you will sleep just right!

They make great companions
And they love to laugh and play.
They stand guard all night
And sleep throughout the day.

You need to meet a yeti!
My mom gave one to me.
It's the fluffiest, cuddliest monster
That you will ever meet!

THIMBLETHOUGHT

Folklorists trace the origin of the Yeti to a combination of factors, including Sherpa folklore and misidentified fauna such as bear or yak. The Yeti is commonly compared to Bigfoot of North America.

WONDERFUZZ

Do good (loving) people and good (loving) pets turn into good (loving) ghosts?

THIMBLETHOUGHT

Scientists say there is no evidence of ghosts, but that our brains are very good at imagining and hallucinating.

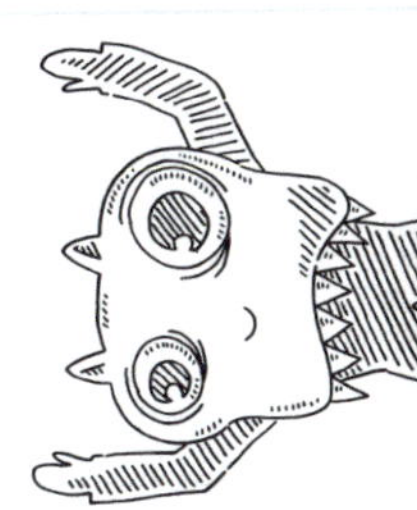

A **stanza** is a group of lines in a poem. A **quatrain** is a four-line stanza.

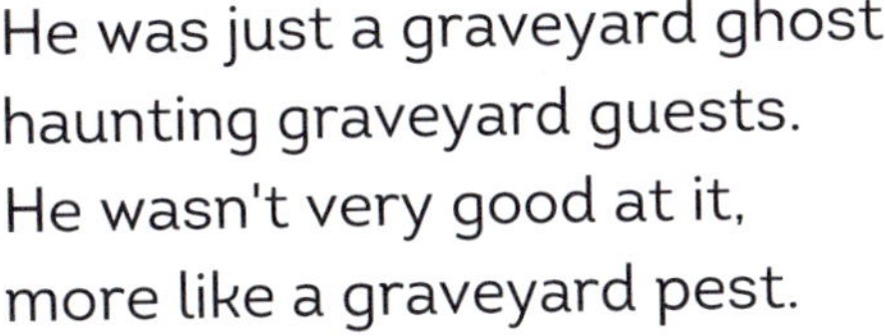

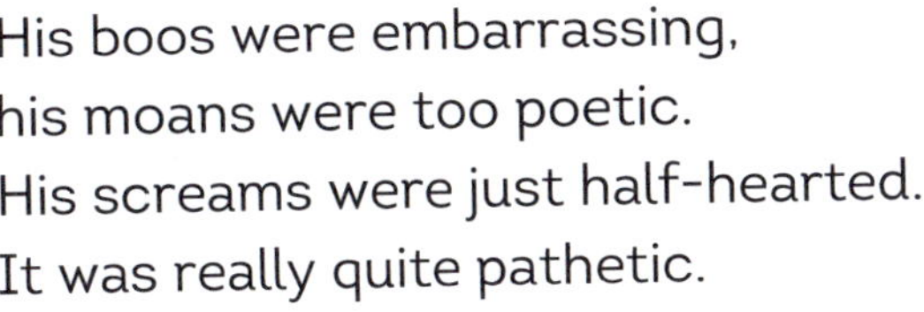

GHOST UNLIKELY

by Kevan Atteberry

He was just a graveyard ghost
haunting graveyard guests.
He wasn't very good at it,
more like a graveyard pest.

His boos were embarrassing,
his moans were too poetic.
His screams were just half-hearted.
It was really quite pathetic.

Yet, he flew around the graveyard
believing he was scary.
When asked if they were frightened,
most people said, "Not very."

Things People Are Afraid Of

Fear of public speaking
Fear of heights
Fear of flying
Fear of spiders
Fear of snakes
Fear of the dark
Fear of injections
Fear of thunder and lightning
Fear of crowds
Fear of germs

A TORNADO'S IN MY TUMMY
by Clara

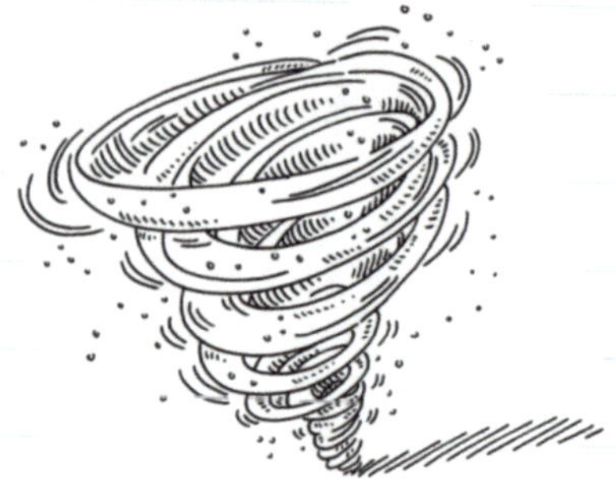

I'm ready to spew lava.
I've never felt this sick.
A tornado's in my tummy.
My brain is full of bricks.
I ate a ton of candy
and a dump-truck load of cake.

Hyperbole = Exaggeration
[Hi **per** bo lee]

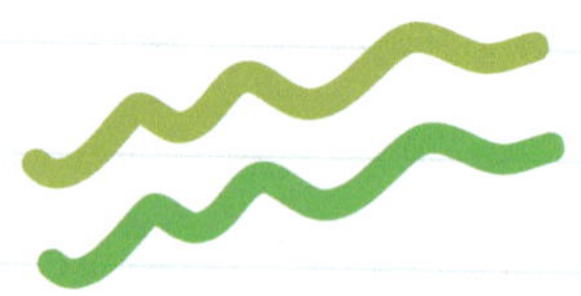

And then a spaceship kidnapped me . . .
This body here's a FAKE!

THIMBLETHOUGHT

World UFO Day is an unofficial holiday celebrated on July 2nd when people share stories and theories.

WONDERFUZZ

I wonder if aliens would ever kidnap us for good and friendly reasons?

Signs That You're Really Sick

- Fever
- No appetite
- Pain
- Rash
- Nausea
- Vomiting
- Hard to breathe
- Pale (paler than usual) skin
- Crying
- Diarrhea
- Sore throat
- Cough
- Fatigue

WONDERFUZZ

Have humans always wondered if there is life on other planets?

THIMBLETHOUGHT

I call them alien spaceships. Mom calls them Unidentified Flying Objects (UFOs). And scientists call them Unidentified Aerial Phenomena (UAPs). Whatever you call them, they're EXCITING!

ALIENS

by Verrena Diane Anderson

A glowing flying saucer hovers
in the evening sky

An orange aura spreads
through the atmosphere

Creepy birds circle above the trees

Ominous voices whisper
inside my head

Are aliens coming after me?

I look
again . . . and shout

Hey, everybody,
the sun looks like a UFO!

Amy's mom makes me drink a cup of bitter tea.
"It will make you better, just you wait and see."
Very soon, close to noon, my nausea is gone.
Who wants cake? I do! Bring it on!

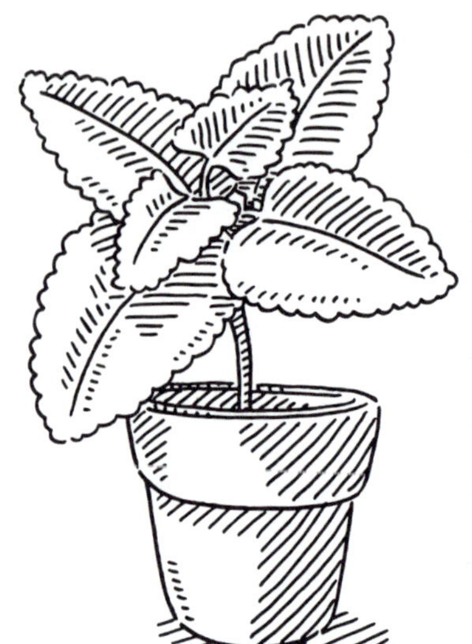

WONDERFUZZ

Mom says dogs eat grass when they feel sick; is this true, or do they just like the taste?

THIMBLE THOUGHT

"Borage" is pronounced like "porridge." For "karpooravalli," you pronounce all the parts: car-poor-uh-volley.

The Indian Borage

by Suma Subramaniam

In my house, Amma grows an herb,
plectranthus amboinicus,
Karpooravalli,
the Indian borage.

It only sees the sun from my window,
but it's fragrant from root to tip.
A soothing balm on burnt skin,
a cure for cold, cough, and chronic asthma.

When the wind roars
and the rain pours,
I pluck the leaves,
and Amma heats them to a concentrated decoction.

She mixes the medicine with milk and recites the herb's story,
giving it wings curved against a wide sky.
And at the heart of it,
I learn about the healing power of its leaves.

THIMBLETHOUGHT

Pigs don't sweat, so they need mud and water to keep cool, which leads to a muddy mess.

BUSTED
by Clara

When I get back home,
everyone is QUIET.
James says,
"You are SO busted!"

I look at my messy room.
I feel ashamed, but
what I want to know is:
Has Mom ever actually
seen a pig sty?

FINISHED

by Megan Litwin

I better be finished
cleaning my room
before my mom gets back.
She handed me a broom and rags
and a garbage sack.
I look up at the heaping mess.
I look down at the bin.
I think I might be
FINISHED . . .
before I even begin.

WONDERFUZZ

Is it true that having a house that is TOO clean can lead to children having more allergies?

WONDERFUZZ

Why do people wear matching socks, anyway?

THIMBLETHOUGHT

Static electricity travels at light speed — over 186,000 miles per second.

CHASE (WILD GOOSE THAT IS!)

by Lynn Street

What's that you say?
You're missing a sock?
We'll help you look.
Behind the clock . . .

It's not in the fishbowl,
the freezer, the fridge,
the birdcage, the mailbox,
or Rover's new dish.

Kitty looks innocent.
The hamster does too.
The vacuum ate it?
There must be some clues . . .

What's that you say?
Our guesses are wrong?
The missing sock's
been here all along –

Stuck to a sweater
with static cling,
The hamster's not guilty!
(That's a good thing.)

Most Commonly Lost Things

- keys
- wallet
- phone
- glasses
- sunglasses
- pens
- umbrella
- gloves
- socks (!)
- jewelry
- hats

WONDERFUZZ

Is it true that people called "fullers" in ancient Rome collected urine from public restrooms and used it for washing clothes?

Laundry Trivia

Astronauts on the International Space Station don't do laundry; they eject their dirty clothes into the atmosphere.

The largest outdoor laundry is in Mumbai, India.

In some countries such as Switzerland, neighbors follow a strict schedule for doing laundry.

Metal irons were invented in China over 1,000 years ago; before that, some people used heated rocks to smooth out hides and clothes.

LAUNDRY

by Vicki Wilke

It's like a tightrope tree to tree
beside our house for all to see.
Sometimes I help on tippytoes,
clip clothespins to our drippy clothes.

Turtlenecks get tightly pinned,
shirtsleeves waving in the wind.
Superhero cape flies high,
bedsheets snap against the sky.

Overalls with holey knees
whip like windsocks in the breeze.
My baseball jersey, number nine,
Freshens up with sun and pine.

Mama's blouses made of silk,
hang by sleepers stained with milk.
Then NO SURPRISE – but please don't stare
at our family's UNDERWEAR!

There are **12 compound words** in this poem: tightrope, sometimes, tippytoes, clothespins, turtlenecks, shirtsleeves, superhero, bedsheets, overalls, windsocks, baseball, underwear.

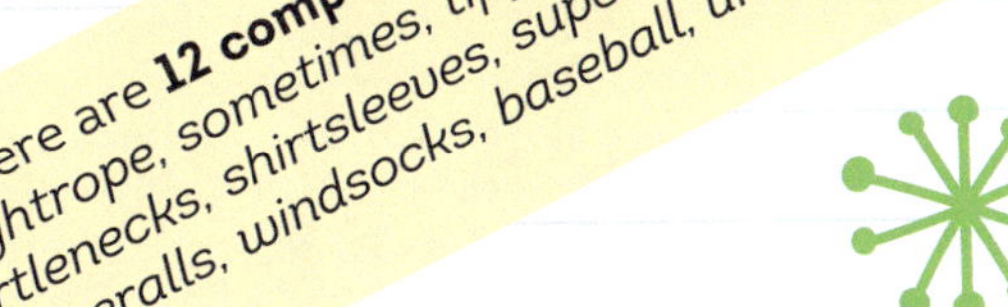

THIMBLETHOUGHT

The ancient Egyptian pharaoh King Tut was buried with 145 pairs of underwear called "schenti" or loincloths to take with him to the underworld.

Errand Dog

by April Halprin Wayland

Well, hello ~
jump inside!
Vroom-vroom-vroom ~
off we ride!

Shop for food,
stop for flowers.
nearly home . . .
this takes hours.

You and me:
good company . . .
one more errand:
run with me!

Now that my room is clean,
I can pay attention to Vera,
who has been shouting,
"Clara! James! Look at Wilby!!"
Wilby is sniffing around
and walking in a circle
and squatting —
HURRY! OUTSIDE!!

WONDERFUZZ

Is this true: if it's 90 degrees outside, leaving your dog in the car for just 10 minutes can be fatal?!

THIMBLETHOUGHT

Most dogs know 165 human words.

UNPLEASANTNESS

by Hollie Dagata

I've heard it said:
"Let sleeping dogs lie."
My little dog's body
could never comply.

He has to go out
to pee and poop,
then it's my job
to clean and scoop.

I love my dog
but I hate that task.
Is there a solution?
I wonder and ask.

Dogs' follow-up vacuums?
Drones that will scoop?
Biodegradable gadgets
that clean up the gloop?

I love my dog, but
I'd rather just play
and skip this unpleasant-
mess
every day.

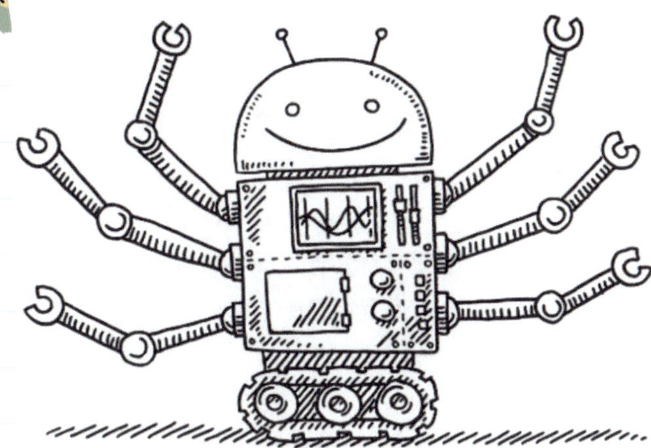

THIMBLETHOUGHT

Caleb Olson invented a smart robotic laser that points out where the piles of dog poop in his yard are — but it's not smart enough to pick them up

PICKING IT UP

by April Halprin Wayland

She pooped by the library,
pooped in the square.
I picked it all up
and now it isn't there!

One great thing about taking Wilby outside is that we get to play while he sniffs around!

HORSESHOES

by Marilyn Garcia

A brother is a bother and a brother is a friend
A brother's an opponent who competes to bitter end
He'll argue
    argue
argue
    argue
argue
    argue AND
pretend his pitch has hit the peg
when all it's hit is sand

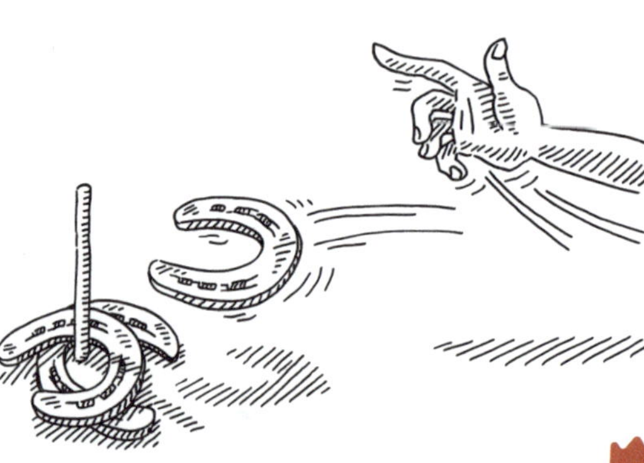

So,
we'll take our shoes and metal stakes and zoom to outer space
where fights float off towards Jupiter and laughter's left in place
'cause on the moon we don't keep track of any points at all –
the fun of lunar horseshoes comes from getting them to
fall

Facts about Horseshoes

The person who makes horseshoes is called a farrier.

Horseshoes are made from iron, rubber, plastic, rawhide, or a combination of these.

A horseshoe is a symbol of good luck.

George W. Bush is an avid player of the game of horseshoes.

THIMBLETHOUGHT

The roots of the game of horseshoes may be found in ancient contests such as the discus throw and quoits.

WONDERFUZZ

Have horseshoes always been made of metal, or have people ever used other materials (leather, plants, etc.)?

Fun Facts about Trees

California has giant sequoia trees that are 4,000–5,000 years old.

Trees absorb carbon dioxide and produce breathable air.

Trees and plants communicate with each other using a massive network of underground fungi called the "wood wide web."

Being around trees is good for our mental health and reducing stress.

WONDERFUZZ

Which animals climb trees (any surprises)?

CEDAR

by Donna JT Smith

A cedar tree stands tall and straight
beside our house. My brother's eight,
and climbs that tree, past limb and twig!
But I'm too scared, I'm not as big.
Up there he points to farmers' crops,
the neighbor's roof, twelve birch treetops,
a robin's nest with four teal eggs;
but all I see are his two legs!
He's even closer to the sun,
while I am farther from the fun!
Someday I'll climb that towering tree
to cedar things that he could see!

THIMBLETHOUGHT

Oil from cedar tree leaves has been used in making perfume, paints, insect spray, and candles, and for creating mummies in ancient Egypt.

PALETERO MAN

by René Saldaña, Jr.

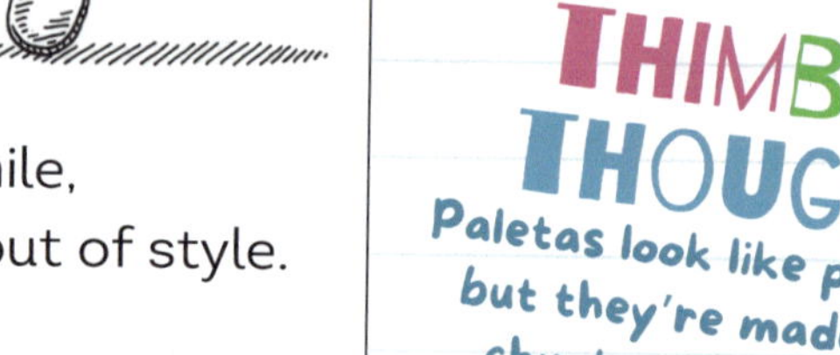

Tling, tling, tling, sing the bells.
Paletas, get your paletas here, he yells.

I got sweet watermelon that'll make you smile,
Some lip-smacking mango that'll never go out of style.

The lemon will make your face go sour,
The tamarind will reveal your superpower.

C'mon out and get your paleta – get one,
Get two, get three. C'mon out and enjoy the sun.

If you can't come to me I'll come to you.
I'll push my paletas all the way to you.

Tling, tling, tling.

Sunday = Funday!
Eat paletas
(popsicles)
and
play, play,
PLAY!

THIMBLE THOUGHT

Paletas look like popsicles, but they're made using chunks of real fruit, vegetables, and even herbs.

WONDERFUZZ

How did we get the word "pickle"ball?

WE WIN!

by Clara

Four of us friends go to the park
to play pickleball (it's not yet dark):
Me and James against Sam and Bob.
Sam serves a pretty good serve, a deep lob.
James returns it. Bob, good get!
I make a drop shot over the net
and we dink — plink — and dink — plunk —
until — oh, no! I pop it up
and WHAM! Sam SLAMS but it's not a slam dunk!
I reset. OK, the ball's still in play.
Bob volleys. James hits it back with spin.
They miss. HOORAY! Game point — we win!

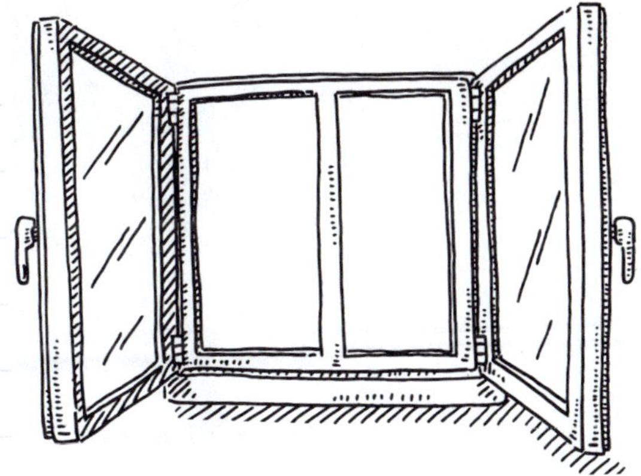

The smell of dinner
floats out our open window.
Oh, no: we are late.
"Better late than never, right?"
Mom's face erases that thought.

This is a **tanka**, an ancient Japanese form that usually has 5 lines with a syllable count of 5-7-5-7-7

Thank You, Mom!

by Janet Clare Fagal

My mother has quite a few sayings.
There are many fish in the sea.
Actions speak louder than words.
These things are confounding to me.

You can't teach an old dog new tricks.
Birds of a feather flock together.
There's another . . . wait . . . I remember!
Better late than never!

WONDERFUZZ

What does it mean when people say "There are many fish in the sea"?

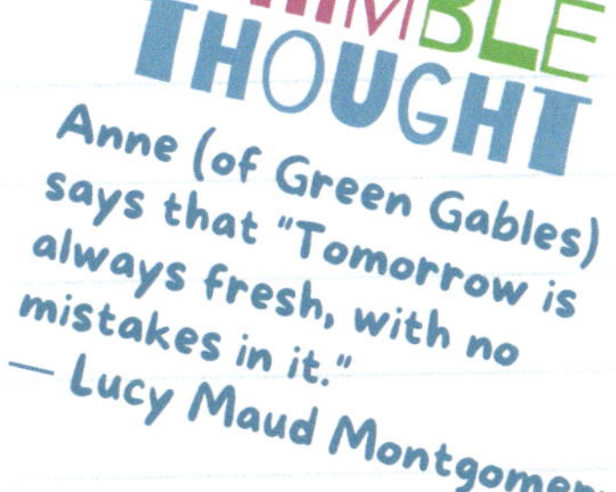

THIMBLE THOUGHT

Anne (of Green Gables) says that "Tomorrow is always fresh, with no mistakes in it."
— Lucy Maud Montgomery

PASTA

by Carmela A. Martino

Every time I eat farfalle,
I get butterflies in my stomach,
and NOT the imaginary kind.
Nonna taught me that farfalle
is the Italian word for butterflies.
Spaghetti means slender strings,
and gemelli are named after twins.

My favorite is vermicelli.
I like sliding the long, skinny noodles around my plate
before scooping some into my mouth. Yum!
But what I love best about vermicelli
is what it means . . .
little worms!

Hmm. I wonder . . .
would vermicelli make good fish bait?

Dear Uncle Frank,

For this poem, maybe you can draw an X-ray of a person whose stomach is full of . . . butterflies!!

**Love,
Clara**

WONDERFUZZ

Is it true that there are more than 350 names in Italian for types of pasta?

THIMBLETHOUGHT

The first pasta factory in the United States was built in Brooklyn, New York, in 1848 by a Frenchman who spread his spaghetti strands on the roof to dry in the sunshine.

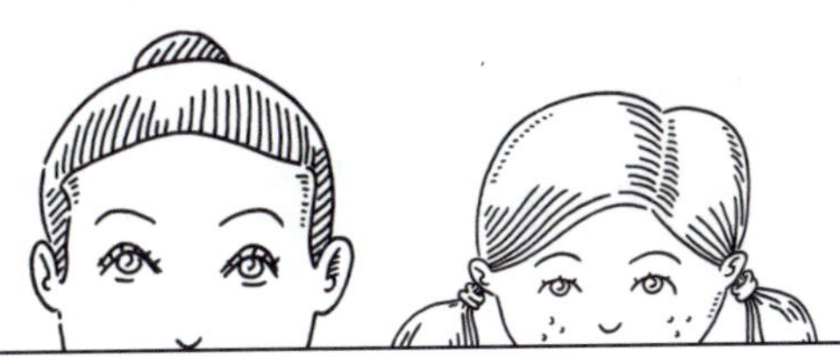

FINISHED?

by Sandy Brehl

My mama's table won't allow for picky eaters' moods.
"Veggies help you grow," she says. "Do not waste this food!"
But cabbage is my nemesis, my nose and mouth refuse it!
The taste is awful and it stinks. Mom says that won't excuse it.

"That's it," she says. "There's no dessert, you're finished for tonight."
I give the cabbage one more look, but I can't take a bite.
"Why no dessert?" I plead my case and wrap up with these facts:
"I'm just too full, but ice cream melts and slides between the cracks!"

Favorite Desserts Around the World

- Pavlova, Australia
- Apfelstrudel, Germany
- Baklava, Greece
- Brownies, United States
- Gelato, Italy
- Bingsoo, Korea
- Cendol, Singapore
- Crème Brûlée, France
- Egg Tarts, Portugal
- Flan, Mexico
- Gulab Jamun, India
- Knafeh, Yemen

THIMBLETHOUGHT

Cabbage can be used to make a simple chemical clock. When a cabbage leaf is dipped in a solution of lemon juice and two different metals (usually zinc and copper), it can generate a small electrical current.

WONDERFUZZ

I hate rhubarb but I L-O-V-E the German song Barbaras Rhabarberbar (Barbara's Rhubarb Bar). If you listen to the song 100 times, it will make you crave rhubarb!

DREAMTIME

by Sara Holbrook

My daydreams blast me into space,
Between the planets
Among the stars,
Way past the moon.
Save me a seat,
I'll be back soon.

Poets love to play with words, especially **puns** that use the double meaning of words (like "pointless") for humor.

WORKS FOR ME

by Cynthia Cotten

I write my poems
with a pen.
Once I used a pencil,
then
the tip broke –
no joke –
and my work became
pointless.

WONDERFUZZ

How fast does a rocket need to go to get into orbit around Earth?

THIMBLETHOUGHT

The average pencil can draw a line that's 35 miles long and write around 45,000 words.

WONDERFUZZ
Are cave paintings the first diaries?

THIMBLETHOUGHT
An average size cedar tree can produce about 300,000 pencils.

MY SERIOUS DIARY AND MY SILLY PENCIL

by Yangsook Choi

I feel at home
however far away I go
if I open my serious diary
and let my silly pencil lead me.
Hey, pencil, get back here! Stop scribbling on my shoe!

My pencil jots down
what I see – *the strange glowworms inside a cave in Australia*
what I ask – *do you pay electric bills, glowworms?*
what I smell – *the smooth monkey poo that fell on my head in Mexico*
what I wonder – *is it a sign for a new shampoo?*
what I hear – *the spotty hyenas' cackling laughs in Tanzania*
what I imagine – *they must be laughing at my helmet*
what I taste – *the slimy frog leg I accidentally gulped in France*
what I feel – *yum! I secretly liked it*
what I touch – *my sweet grandma's hand in Korea*
what I whisper – *I love you . . .*

until it draws the line and goes to sleep
just like at home . . .

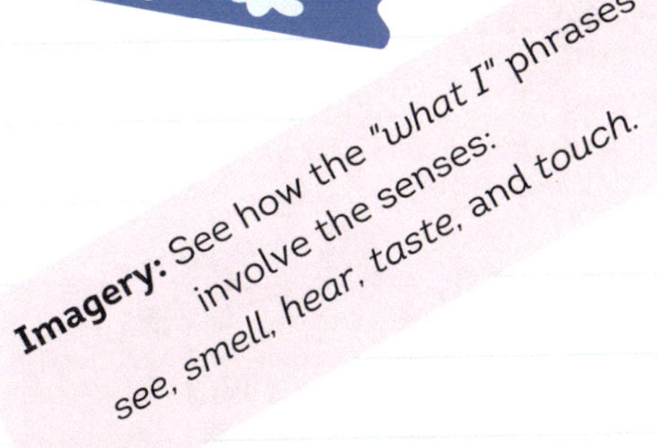

Time Is Winning

by Janet Wong

Time, you're winning.
My head is spinning.
It feels so strange, it sounds so weird
but somehow last week DISAPPEARED.
I had a lot of chores to do.
I frittered a morning away with the flu.
Eating dinner took ten hours
and I spent six more on baths and showers.
Homework gobbled time – a ton!
And I *had* to have a *little* fun,
so I played some video games each night –
Minecraft and, of course, Fortnite –
and I went to a party
and I ran with my dog
and I learned to dance like a big bullfrog.
And I baked some cookies.
And I played pickleball . . .

Well, I guess I did do a LOT, after all!

WONDERFUZZ

Does time go by more quickly as we get older?

THIMBLE THOUGHT

Scientists say that time only moves in one direction — forward, not backward (so far) — but scientists are still studying time!

The Weekend Worked!

by Your Energized Teacher

The weekend worked wonders.
Despite the thunder,
I'm refreshed, refueled,
and newly bejeweled
(thanks to a trip to the mall).
How about y'all?

Mrs. Booker has a Monday Morning poem she wants to share with us . . .

New Week

by Mary E. Cronin

Monday – a new week.
Wipe the slate clean!
All that yuck from last week?
I washed it down the drain.

My math mistakes, that spelling test,
tripping on the stage?
Monday, you're my hero.
Mondays turn the page!

THIMBLETHOUGHT

The word "Monday" comes from an Old English word that means "Moon's day," based on the ancient Roman tradition of naming each day of the week after a celestial body.

WONDERFUZZ

Are there any languages that just use numbers for the days of the week (First-Day, Second-Day, etc.)?

This compendium is due today,
but Mrs. Booker says
that if we want to keep on
doing a compendium
or even "just a junk journal"
of our own (with little tidbits we want to keep),
she will give us each
ANOTHER brand-new notebook.

We can put
important facts or trivia in it
and questions or quotes
and poems or stories
and
of course . . .
ANYTHING we want!

THIMBLETHOUGHT

The most famous journal ever is The Diary of a Young Girl written by Anne Frank when she was in hiding during World War II. It has sold 31 million copies in 67 languages.

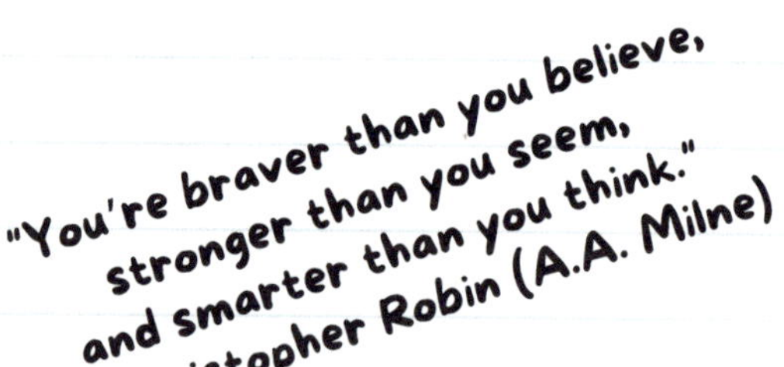

WONDERFUZZ

Each of the DIARY OF A WIMPY KID books has the same number of pages (217) . . . If I work all year, I wonder if I can make a diary - journal - compendium with 217 pages too?

WONDERFUZZ

Is it true that WONDERING can make us happier?

My Thoughts

by Eric Ode

I think of grumpy thunderstorms
that shake a winter sky,
and shooting stars that light the night,
then vanish when they die.
I think of skitter-scatter crabs
in crusty, armored shells,
and bullfrog songs that croak and creak
as deep as wishing wells.

I keep these thoughts and wonders
in this journal of my own,
a place to hide my questions,
and a place that's mine alone –
my thoughts of frogs and crawling crabs
and shooting stars and thunder,
and thoughts of why I wonder
why I wonder
what I wonder.

THIMBLETHOUGHT

Shooting stars are actually called meteors and move so fast that they glow as they head toward Earth.

IT'S NOT THAT I'M SO SMART,
IT'S JUST THAT
I STAY WITH PROBLEMS
LONGER.

— ALBERT EINSTEIN

Awesome Activities
For Ravenous Writers

In this section of the book you'll find:

1) awesome **activities for kids** (especially kids who love to write); find more activity sheets like these at PomeloBooks.com;

2) a handy list of the **writing exercises** in this book;

3) **indexes, poem credits,** and **poet bios**;

4) **info about the creators** of this book; and

5) recommendations for **other poetry books** by this creative team!

Fun Things To Do

1. **Keep a journal**
2. **Research fun facts**
3. **Doodle**
4. **Take photos**
5. **Share family stories and memories – then write them down**

To Stretch Your Mind

6. **Look up quotes**
7. **Find poems & share them**
8. **Make lists**
9. **Jot down wonderfuzz questions**
10. **Link poetry + thimblethoughts**

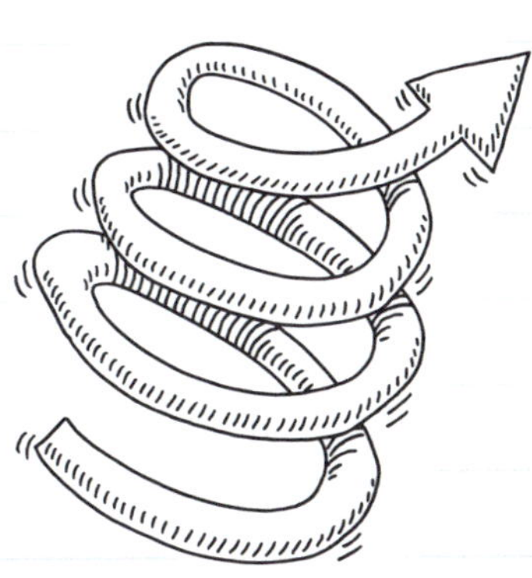

See page 16 of *Clara's Kooky's Compendium of Thimblethoughts and Wonderfuzz*

EXERCISE #5: FAMILY

Find pictures or drawings of some of your family members and write about them.

See page 18 of *Clara's Kooky's Compendium of Thimblethoughts and Wonderfuzz*

EXERCISE #6: PETS

Write about pets you have or have had – or wish you had.

See page 26 of *Clara's Kooky's Compendium of Thimblethoughts and Wonderfuzz*

EXERCISE #8: FRIENDS

Write about some of your friends (nearby or far away, "real" or "imaginary").

Clara's example

I have school friends, neighborhood friends, soccer friends, basketball friends, pickleball friends, and friends who know me because of Mom and Uncle Frank. I'm putting Vera and James here in my friends circle too because you can be friends with your family, right?

ME

See page 34 of *Clara's Kooky's Compendium of Thimblethoughts and Wonderfuzz*

EXERCISE #10: FAVORITE FOOD

Do you have a favorite food (at school or at home)? Write about it.

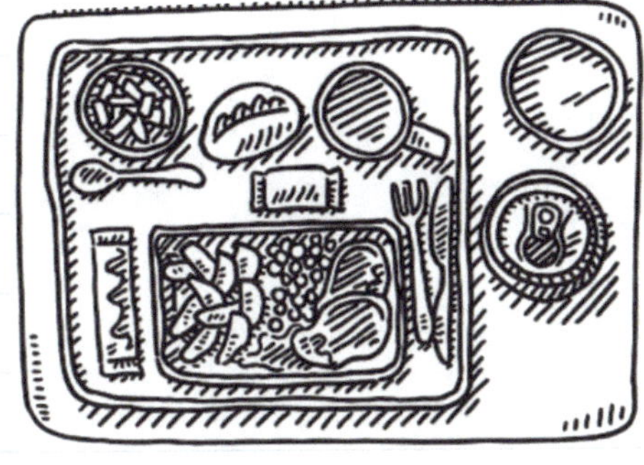

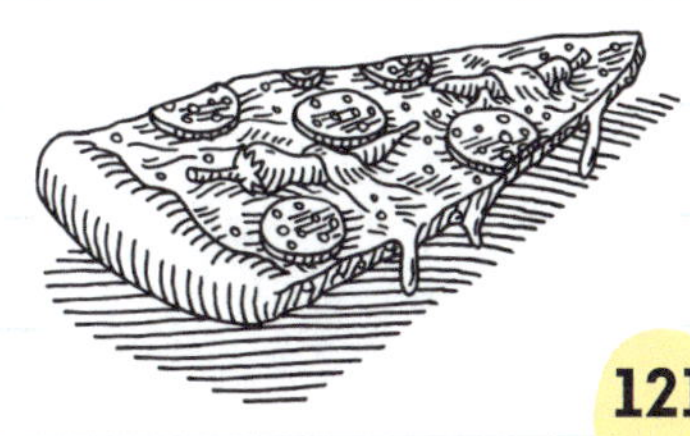

See page 42 of *Clara's Kooky's Compendium of Thimblethoughts and Wonderfuzz*

EXERCISE #14: AFTER SCHOOL

What do you like to do AFTER school? Write about it.

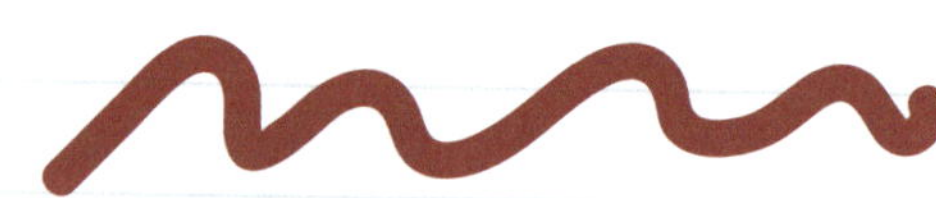

See page 48 of *Clara's Kooky's Compendium of Thimblethoughts and Wonderfuzz*

EXERCISE #15: WORD HUNT

Write a poem that uses homophones or homographs or any kind of wordplay.

homograph = two words that are spelled the same but have different sounds and meanings

I,
eye!

The HORSE is
HOARSE!
Hay - hey!
No way —
no weigh!!
I love
homophones!!

homophone = two words that sound the same but have different spellings and meanings

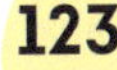

See page 76 of *Clara's Kooky's Compendium of Thimblethoughts and Wonderfuzz*

EXERCISE #19: DREAM JOBS

What are some jobs that you might like? Be daring! Be creative! Think BIG!

WRITING EXERCISES

Exercise #1: Author Bio (p. 6)
Put a picture or drawing of yourself in your compendium. Write your author bio and add it to your book.

Exercise #2: Poet List (p. 10)
Keep a list of names of poets whose poems you like. Look for poems by them to print and tape into YOUR compendium.

Exercise #3: Questions (p. 12)
Keep a list of questions about things you wonder about.

Exercise #4: Word Bank (p. 14)
Make a list of words that are interesting to you. You can look them up in a dictionary and try using them in your writing.

Exercise #5: Family (p. 16)
Find pictures or drawings of some of your family members and write about them.

Exercise #6: Pets (p. 18)
Write about pets you have or have had – or wish you had.

Exercise #7: Neighbors (p. 22)
Write about some of your neighbors (or their pets).

Exercise #8: Friends (p. 26)
Write about some of your friends (nearby or far away, "real" or "imaginary").

Exercise #9: Getting to School (p. 30)
Do you walk to school? Ride the bus? Does someone drive you? Write about it.

Exercise #10: Favorite Food (p. 34)
Do you have a favorite food (at school or at home)? Write about it.

Exercise #11: Worries (p. 36)
Are there things (big or small) you worry about? Write about it!

Exercise #12: Math Intersections (p. 38)
Write about something you've learned about in math this year.

Exercise #13: Science Explorations (p. 40)
Write about something you've learned about in science this year.

Exercise #14: After School (p. 42)
What do you like to do AFTER school? Write about it.

Exercise #15: Word Hunt (p. 48)
Write a poem that uses homophones or homographs or any kind of wordplay.

Exercise #16: Wild Animals (p. 52)
Make a list of wild animals. Find a poem and 3 or more facts about one you choose.

Exercise #17: Social Studies Connections (p. 70)
Write about something you've learned about in social studies (geography, history, etc.) this year.

Exercise #18: Jobs in Our Community (p. 72)
Write about the jobs that some of the people you know have.

Exercise #19: Dream Jobs (p. 76)
What are some jobs that you might like? Be daring! Be creative! Think BIG!

Exercise #20: On Your Own (p. 81)
Write about something happening in your life outside of school.

Subject Index

Poet Index with Titles & Credits

These poems are used with the permission of the author, with all rights reserved. To request reprint rights, please send an email to info@pomelobooks.com and we'll connect you with the poets.

Melander, Rochelle: "Chickenosaurus" (p. 58); "Toot!" (p. 62); © 2024 by Rochelle Melander.

Mihaly, Christy: "Just Wondering" (p. 13); © 2024 by Christy Mihaly.

Milholland, Amy: "My Teacher Has a Fish Tank TV" (p. 50); © 2024 by Amy Milholland.

Moore, Kate McCarroll: "Test Dread" (p. 36); © 2024 by Kate McCarroll Moore.

Nesbitt, Kenn: "My Robot Is Awesome!" (p. 41); © 2024 by Kenn Nesbitt.

Norton, Elisabeth: "Outerwear" (p. 57); © 2024 by Elisabeth Norton.

Ode, Eric: "In This Journal" (p. 7); "My Thoughts" (p. 115); © 2024 by Eric Ode.

Oqueli, Abby: "Have You Ever Met a Yeti?" (p. 94); © 2024 by Abby Oqueli.

Peterson, Eric E.: "Career Day" (p. 74); "Help Wanted?" (p. 72); © 2024 by Eric E. Peterson.

Reidy, Deborah: "Homework" (p. 42); "Pirate" (p. 42); © 2024 by Deborah S. Reidy.

Renauld, Laura: "Pet" (p. 87); "Wild" (p. 55); © 2024 by Laura Renauld.

Riordan, Joan: "How to Eat at a Swanky Restaurant with Your Friend's Family (If You Never Want to Be Invited Again)*" (p. 88); "I Know Mom Will Probably Say No But . . ." (p. 21); © 2024 by Joan Riordan.

Saldaña, René, Jr.: "Paletero Man" (p. 106); © 2024 by René Saldaña, Jr.

Salinger, Michael: "Where Does the Sky Begin?" (p. 12); © 2024 by Michael Salinger.

Sardelli, Darren: "Behind the Hidden Door" (p. 43); © 2024 by Darren Sardelli.

Smith, Donna JT: "Cedar" (p. 105); "Nay" (p. 48); © 2024 by Donna JT Smith.

Spinelli, Eileen: "Table Manners 101" (p. 89); "The Art of Apologizing After Hurting a Friend" (p. 69); © 2024 by Eileen Spinelli.

Steinglass, Elizabeth: "Please Pay Attention" (p. 79); © 2024 by Elizabeth Steinglass.

Street, Lynn: "Chase (Wild Goose That Is!)" (p. 100); © 2024 by Lynn Street.

Subramaniam, Suma: "The Indian Borage" (p. 98); © 2024 by Suma Subramaniam.

Tarantino, Linda Picaro: "Who 8 the Candy?" (p. 82); © 2024 by Linda Picaro Tarantino.

Taylor, Pamela: "Stink!" (p. 90); © 2024 by Pamela Taylor.

Thomas, Linda Jean: "Vampire-ish" (p. 56); © 2024 by Linda Jean Thomas.

Uglow, Joyce: "AKA" (p. 18); "RSVP" (p. 81); © 2024 by Joyce Uglow.

Valentino, Fernanda: "Mighty Apostrophe" (p. 51); © 2024 by Fernanda Valentino.

Varsalona, Carol: "Would You Like to Bake?" (p. 83); © 2024 by Carol Varsalona.

Venkatraman, Padma: "Job Juggler" (p. 75); © 2024 by Padma Venkatraman.

Waters, Charles: "Clara's Got the Lunchie Munchies" (p. 34); © 2024 by Charles Waters.

Wayland, April Halprin: "Errand Dog" (p. 102); "Picking It Up" (p. 103); © 2024 by April Halprin Wayland.

Wilke, Vicki: "Laundry" (p. 101); "Rain" (p. 87); © 2024 by Vicki Wilke.

Wolf, Allan: "Lunchroom Virtuosos" (p. 35); "Playing Attention" (p. 78); © 2024 by Allan Wolf.

Wong, Janet: "Assembly Behavior" (p. 78); "Jibber-Jabber" (p. 31); "Slumber Party To-Do List" (p. 92); "Time Is Winning" (p. 112). Also, text in the voice of Clara, including these and other titled or untitled poems by Clara or Clara's Toes: "A Tornado's in My Tummy" (p. 96); "A Terror of Tyrannosaurs" (p. 58); "Breaking into a Smile" (p. 32); "Busted" (p. 99); "Cicada-Head?! Really?!!!" (p. 68); "Dear Elise" (p. 69);"Elise Is a Cicada-Head" (p. 67); "Formula for a Rainout" (p. 87); "Four Kids on a Patio" (p. 90); "free" (p. 51); "Harry Has a Cell Phone" (p. 32); "How Now Brown Sow" (p. 49); "How to Chitter-Chatter" (p. 31); "James's Brain Is Zooming" (p. 78); "Laws of Our Family" (p. 20); "My Brother the Rocket" (p. 78); "My Robot" (p. 41); "Porcupine Math" (p. 50); "Research" (p. 53); "Stupid" (p. 39); "Teamwork Gone Berserk" (p. 67); "The Morning Rush Has Mom in a Tizzy" (p. 28); "They're There Again?" (p. 27); "This Is My ~~Journal~~ Compendium" (p. 8); untitled haiku ("Birds can fly away") (p. 87); untitled tanka ("The smell of dinner" (p. 107); "VERA" (p. 16); "We Win!" (p. 106); "What Is a Poem?" (p. 10); "Your Woes" (p. 91); text in the voice of Elise: "Dear Clara" (p. 69); and text in the voice of Mrs. Booker, "Your Energized Teacher," "Your Tired Teacher": "Test-Taking Tips" (p. 37); "The Weekend Worked!" (p. 112); and "Weakened Before the Weekend" (p. 80); © 2024 by Janet S. Wong.

Zax, Helen Kemp: "Butt" (p. 62); "Pointer" (p. 34); "Yackety-Yacker" (p. 54); © 2024 by Helen Kemp Zax.

Zoells, Darcy Day: "Ostrich" (p. 60); © 2024 by Darcy Day Zoells.

About The Poets

Alma Flor Ada (almaflorada.com) is a poet with a poetic name. In Spanish, Alma means Soul, Flor means Flower, and her last name Ada means Fairy. She always answers YES! with a smile when people ask her if that is her true name.

Verrena Diane Anderson (newtreemom.wordpress.com) is a retired ESL teacher and lifelong reader who wonders how long it will take to read all the books at the new branch of her local library.

Dolores Andral (doloresandral.com) is a writer and sometimes illustrator who can only draw stick figures, but believes that counts for something.

Marcie Flinchum Atkins (marcieatkins.com) is a teacher-librarian by day and a noticer of small surprising things in nature on weekends.

Kevan Atteberry (kevanatteberry.com) is a writer and illustrator of books for kids. He loves banana cream pie and the color periwinkle, and was once bitten by a raven.

Lisa Billa (X: @lisasbilla) writes especially for children. It would be hard for her to choose a favorite animal, but some of her current fiction projects feature tortoises, pangolins, banana slugs, otters, and manatees, who definitely deserve more stories.

Robyn Hood Black (robynhoodblack.com) is a poet, writer, and artist who wonders why her brother got all the math genes.

Merry Bradshaw (cedarpocketpress.com) is a former teacher, principal, and curriculum director. Currently, she is a children's writer and poet who wonders why tomatoes, lemons, peaches, and grapes are the same color inside and out but watermelon is green on the outside and red on the inside.

Jay Brazeau (IG: @theotherjaybrazeau) is a poet from Ottawa, Canada who wonders if horses are really as hungry as we think they are.

Sandy Brehl (SandyBrehlBooks.com) is a reader, writer, thinker, and educator enthralled with ENGLISH – an astonishingly rich and versatile language, but also a dirty, rotten troublemaker. Right? Write? Rite?

Calef Brown (calefbrown.com) is an artist, poet, and educator who wonders why he can understand Flaubert best when wearing a secondhand mohair vest.

F. Isabel Campoy (isabelcampoy.com) hides a first name in that F. The true meaning, she says, is: Forever a Funny Fabulous Fantastic Friend of children (and also Francisca).

Yangsook Choi (yangsookchoi.com) is a children's author and illustrator who plays percussion with a pencil and a chopstick on an empty tuna can to get the right rhythm of a poem.

Cynthia Cotten (cynthiacotten.com) has been writing fiction and poetry most of her life. Two of her favorite wonderings are "why?" and "why not?"

Mary E. Cronin (maryecronin.com) is a poet, children's book author, and K-3 Literacy Coach who feels a sense of wonder in large and beautiful libraries.

Hollie Dagata is a retired elementary school teacher who wonders why the lines in our lives don't always rhyme.

Leslie Degnan (southern-breeze.org/leslie-ross-degnan.html) is a writer of picture books and poetry for children who wonders why keeping your head in the clouds while getting your ducks in a row is so much fun.

Kristy Dempsey (kristydempsey.com) is a former K-12 librarian and English teacher who wonders if the owl, the fox, and the possum who visit her yard are friends.

Joanne Emery (WordDancerBlog.com) is a teacher, poet, artist, and forever-dreamer who has decided never to retire or grow old!

Margarita Engle (margaritaengle.com) is convinced that dogs can smell time, because they always know exactly when to start reminding us to feed them, walk them, or wake up, wake up, wake up!

Janet Clare Fagal (facebook.com/janet.clare.311) is a retired teacher, a poet, and a Grandma. She often wonders if she could become a cool singer or a painter and wants to know how we get our talents.

Douglas Florian (douglasflorian.com) is a poet and a painter who rigorously conforms to non-conformity.

Patricia J. Franz (patriciajfranz.com) is a children's author and poet who wonders if birds begin singing when dawn breaks or if dawn breaks when birds begin singing.

Marilyn Garcia (marilynrgarcia.com) is a poet-scientist and curious creative who wonders why her cats get comfy in every rectangle except the cozy cat beds she buys for them.

Van G. Garrett (vanggarrettpoet.com) is the author of KICKS, a picture book that is a love letter to sneakerheads young and old. Van wonders if Rusty, his always-munching guinea pig, ever gets tired of grazing on hay and healthy treats . . .

Charles Ghigna (FatherGoose.com) is probably the only poet on the planet over the age of twelve who is happy not to have a cell phone.

Avis Harley (poetryfoundation.org/poets/avis-harley) is a teacher-poet, and when the yearly School Photo Day begins, / her kids love finding words that capture their grins, but NO CHEESE, PLEASE!

David L. Harrison (davidlharrison.com) is Missouri's Poet Laureate and a children's writer who wonders why some plants are flowers and some are weeds and who gets to decide.

Jane Heitman Healy (X: @janemhealy) is a poet and writer who talks to backyard birds in their language and wonders what she's saying.

Sara Holbrook (saraholbrook.com) is rarely focused on just one thing: a poet, performer, teacher, world traveler, quilter, and haphazard gardener, she writes for kids of all ages.

Lyn Jekowsky (X: @ljekowsky) is a children's writer, gardener, animal lover, and beach aficionado who wonders what her peonies say to each other, as their beautiful blossoms are so short-lived.

Alan Katz (alankatz.com) loves cantaloupe and the New York Mets, but has never had a pickle or a cup of tea. He and his amazing wife Rose have four amazing kids who each do amazing things. Alan also needs a new thesaurus.

Julie Larios (booksaroundthetable.wordpress.com/author/julielarios) is a poet for children and adults. Growing up, she was the baby of her family, too - just like Vera. And even as a grown-up, she wiggles, squeaks, and shouts.

Irene Latham (irenelatham.com) is a poet from Alabama who wonders if spore-speckled fern fronds know they're beautiful.

Megan Litwin (meganlitwinbooks.com) is a former-yet-forever teacher who now writes picture books, poetry, early readers, and messy lists . . . and wonders about words all day long.

Molly Lorenz (X: @booksR4me) is a children's writer from Pennsylvania. She thinks it would be funny if animals could do all the artsy things an artist does.

George Ella Lyon (georgeellalyon.com) is a poet who writes for readers of all ages. When she was a kid, she and her best friend had a Cat Rescue Society. For a quarter, they would go anywhere to save your cat. Once they got paid in kittens!

J. David Martinez is a teacher and future librarian who wonders: Do pigeons sleep in a nest of French fries?

Carmela A. Martino (carmelamartino.com) is a poet, novelist, and writing teacher who wonders if robins prefer eating vermicelli with or without pasta sauce.

Former elementary teacher **Sara Matson** (saramatson.com) is a children's writer who wonders why she's the only person she knows who doesn't like watermelon.

Rochelle Melander (writenowcoach.com) is an author, writing and ADHD coach, and artist educator who teaches her students tortoise skills: take small steps, dance in the rain, and brumate once a year.

Christy Mihaly (christymihaly.com) is a children's author and poet who wonders how birds find their way when they migrate, and whatever happened to that brilliant idea that came in the middle of the night.

Amy Milholland (amymilholland.com) is an artist, teacher, poet, and musician who wonders what her toddler Max is thinking when he's sitting in his high chair and eating his mac and cheese while staring out the window, looking very pleased and also like he's deeply thinking.

Kate McCarroll Moore (katemccarrollmoore.com) is a poet and children's book author who wonders whatever happened to the imaginary horse she used to ride.

Kenn Nesbitt (poetry4kids.com) is a professional daydreamer and former US Children's Poet Laureate who wonders what that giant, hairy creature right behind you is.

Elisabeth Norton (elisabethnorton.com) is a writer and English teacher who, like a decorator crab, loves decorating – but not with seaweed or sponges!

Eric Ode (ericode.com) is a poet and songwriter who frequently wonders if whatever he's up to at the moment is really such a good idea.

Abby Oqueli (mrsoqueli@edublogs.org) is a secondary English teacher and Librarian who wonders why all things don't begin with alliteration and all poems don't rhyme!?!?!

Eric E. Peterson (petersonfineart.com) is a peculiar, pickle-loving, persnickety person who periodically ponders potential poetic pieces for publication.

Deborah Reidy (linkedin.com/in/deborah-reidy-lab979b9/) is a children's poet and former teacher who wonders, and is asking for a friend, "Is eating a lot of raw chocolate chip cookie dough really that bad for you?"

Laura Renauld (laurarenauld.com) is a children's author and Earth care enthusiast who wonders if she has met a future climate scientist at one of her school visits.

Joan Riordan (X: @JRiordan173) is a walker, a baker, and a poetry maker. She'd rather have to shoo flies occasionally than shoe them.

René Saldaña, Jr. (renesaldanajr.blogspot.com) grew up eating helados and paletas, his all-time favorite being the pineapple, lime a close second. Grown up, he still eats them and writes poems about them.

Michael Salinger (michaelsalinger.com) is a poet, cyclist, metal artist, and father who travels the world with his partner in rhyme Sara Holbrook, helping teachers find ways to use poetry every day in their classroom.

Darren Sardelli (LaughAlotPoetry.com) is an animated poet and author who's convinced that popcorn gives him superpowers.

Donna JT Smith (mainelywrite.blogspot.com) is a retired teacher and a forever poet who wonders if stars are really little pinholes showing bits of light through the night curtain.

Eileen Spinelli (eileenspinelli.com) is a grandma, writer, and bird lover who wonders what it would be like to be friends with a crow.

Elizabeth Steinglass (elizabethsteinglass.com) is a poet who wonders why move, love, and stove have the same spelling pattern but are pronounced differently.

Lynn Street (lynnstreetbooks.com) is a science-inspired children's author and poet who wonders where her missing socks and mittens go.

Suma Subramaniam (sumasubramaniam.com) is a poet and children's author who imagines that writing and gardening have their own natural rhythm for coming to life no matter how fast we want them to bloom.

Linda Picaro Tarantino is a poet, an artist, and a former professor and wonders if adults read funny and kooky poetry like kids, would they enjoy poetry more?

Pamela Taylor (pamelabtaylor.com) is a children's poet and writer who wonders why ladybugs are all ladybugs and not both ladybugs and gentlemanbugs. She wonders why the biggest creatures on earth eat the smallest kinds of food and still grow so huge!

Linda Jean Thomas (lindajthomas.com) is a writer and dabbler in arts and crafts who wonders every morning, "What will I create today – a poem, a painting, or a pop-up card?"

Joyce Uglow (aka JPU; joyceuglowauthor.com) is a picture book author and poet obsessed with unearthing wondrous information about the natural world.

Fernanda Valentino (X: @fgvalentino) is a poet who grew up in Australia and wonders if living upside down has affected her in any way . . .

Carol Varsalona (X: @cvarsalona) is a former school district administrator, adjunct professor, ELA consultant, and current poet who wonders if she will ever master her grandmother's and mother's baking techniques.

Padma Venkatraman (padmavenkatraman.com) is a poet, novelist, and oceanographer who wonders why nights fall and mornings break.

Charles Waters (charleswaterspoetry.com) is a children's poet, author, anthologist, and actor who wonders why more conflicts can't be resolved by sharing a good meal, followed by watching videos of laughing infants.

April Halprin Wayland (aprilwayland.com) hikes, sings songs, and fights to right wrongs. She's ½ author, ½ poet, and ½ not good at fractions.

Vicki Wilke (winningwriters.com/people/vicki-wilke) has loved and written poetry her entire life. She hopes to continue strewing words across the page, for every age.

All night long, poet and author **Allan Wolf** (allanwolf.com) wondered where the sun had gone. Then, in the morning, it finally dawned on him.

Helen Kemp Zax (helenzax.com) is a children's author and poet who would love to write a sonnet about her favorite fruit – but, sadly, no words rhyme with "orange."

Darcy Day Zoells (DarcyDayZoells.com) is a poet and illustrator who likes to tell stories with pictures and draw pictures with words.

About Sylvia Vardell + Janet Wong

Sylvia M. Vardell is Professor Emerita in the School of Library and Information Studies at Texas Woman's University where she taught graduate courses in children's and young adult literature for more than 20 years. Vardell has published extensively, including five books on literature for children as well as over 25 book chapters and 100 journal articles. The Wilby in this book is actually HER dog and they take a daily walk to see his best friend, Wilson, a Corgi who lives down the block. Learn more about Sylvia at SylviaVardell.com.

Janet Wong is a graduate of Yale Law School and a former lawyer. She has written more than 40 books for children on a wide variety of subjects, including chess (*Alex and the Wednesday Chess Club*) and yoga (*Twist: Yoga Poems*). She is the 2021 winner of the NCTE Excellence in Poetry for Children Award, a lifetime achievement award that is one of the highest honors a children's poet can receive. Janet's favorite thing to do (and watch and talk about) is pickleball. Working on this book made her skip playing about 2,673 pickleball games, but immediately upon finishing this book she jumped right back into it to make up all that lost time. Learn more about Janet at Janet-Wong.com.

Together, Vardell & Wong are the creative forces behind Pomelo Books, a publisher whose anthologies feature the work of more than 250 poets.

About Frank Ramspott

Frank Ramspott is a professional artist from Munich, Germany who studied communication design and fashion graphics at Deutsche Meisterschule fuer Mode in Munich and worked for five years as an art director at an advertising agency. For more than 20 years he has been a freelance graphic designer and illustrator whose work can be found on iStockphoto and Getty Images. You can also find his drawings in *The Poetry of Science*, an anthology of 248 poems published by Pomelo Books. Frank loves drawing animals, people, and everything he sees on his travels.

About Pomelo Books

Pomelo Books is Poetry PLUS. Poetry PLUS play. Poetry PLUS science. Poetry PLUS holidays. Poetry PLUS pets – and more. We make it EASY and FUN to share poetry anytime!

The anthologies we have published contain nearly 1,000 poems by 250+ poets on a wide variety of topics and in a wide variety of voices. We're proud to have worked with a "who's who" of children's poets over the years, in addition to several award-winning poets *before* they won their awards. Our real coup, though, has been introducing the work of many brand-new poets who are definitely destined for fame and fortune (well, by poets' standards).

We like to say, "There's a poem for that." And there truly is: on whatever topic you need, for whatever occasion, there is a poem you can enjoy. There's also "a poet for you." If you are an educator or simply an active parent volunteer, you can use this book and our other anthologies to find poets to invite to your school. Most established poets charge a speaking fee of at least $500 per assembly, but there are many poets (including poets who are experienced educators) who would be willing to work with children in your classroom for as little as $100. If you'd like to invite three or four poets over the course of a year in a "poet-in-residence" program, reach out to us on social media and we can put you in touch with the poets who can meet your needs.

Best Books for Brain Breaks

HOP TO IT: Poems to Get You Moving
A Kids' Book Choice Award "Best Book of Facts" Winner

This anthology of 100 poems by 90 poets gets kids thinking and moving as they use pantomime, sign language, and whole body movements, including deskercise! You'll also find the classic "getting the wiggles out" poem "Can You Wiggle Like a Worm?" by Rose Cappelli, and poems for mindfulness such as "Zen Tree" by Margaret Simon.

Take a 30-second indoor recess whenever you need it!

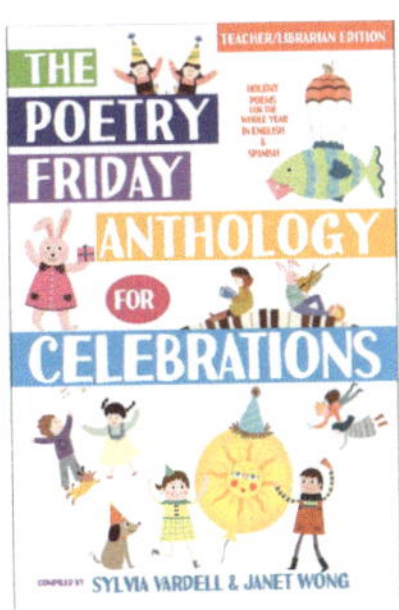

The Poetry Friday Anthology for Celebrations
ILA Notable Books for a Global Society

This fun book features 156 poems (in both Spanish & English) honoring a wide variety of traditional and non-traditional holidays from all over the world. Get set to celebrate birthdays, Talk Like a Pirate Day, Pizza Week, Dinosaur Month, and a whole lot more! Available in a Teacher/Librarian Edition (with a Take 5! mini-lesson for each poem) or in a children's edition.

"A bubbly and educational bilingual poetry anthology for children." – Kirkus

The Poetry of Science
An NSTA Recommends selection

The Poetry of Science is an illustrated book for children that contains 250 poems on science, technology, engineering, and math organized by topic. A K-5 Teacher/Librarian edition, *The Poetry Friday Anthology for Science*, provides connections to topics outlined in the Next Generation Science Standards.

"A treasury of the greatest science poetry for children ever written, with a twist." – NSTA

Best Books for Young Writers

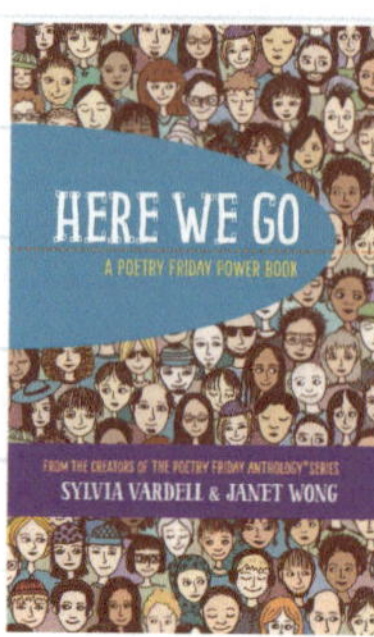

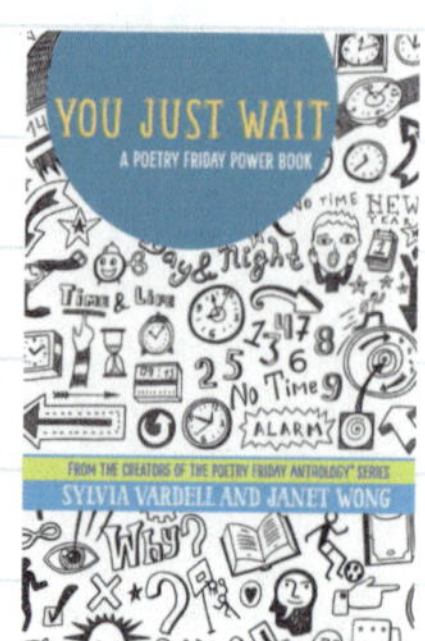

Pet Crazy - Here We Go - You Just Wait

NCTE Poetry Notables

An NNSTOY Social Justice Book *(Here We Go)*

The books in this Poetry Friday Power Book series tell a story in poems. *Pet Crazy* (for younger readers) features pets; *Here We Go* (for middle grades) involves kids who want to make the world a better place; and *You Just Wait* (for tweens and teens) is about sports, food, movies, and identity. The books contain PowerPack activities for young writers.

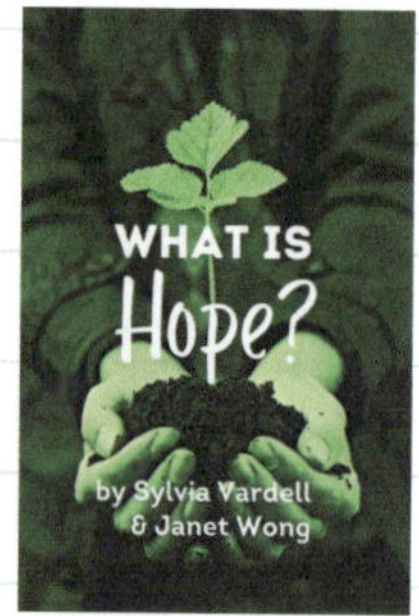

What Is a Friend?
What Is a Family?
What Is Hope?

CBC Hot Off the Press selections

IBBY Fundraiser Books

The three books in this series of ekphrastic poems explore the many aspects of friendship, family, and hope. Young writers will find inspiration in poems written about black-and-white photographs depicting teammates as friends, friends who are family, pets, and the many everyday situations where hope helps us get through the day.

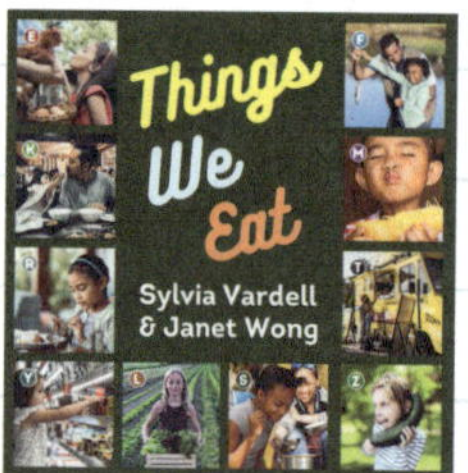

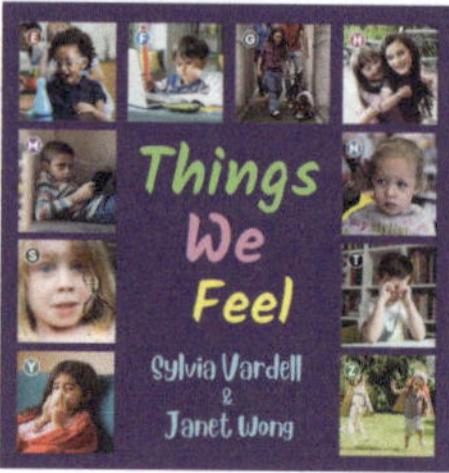

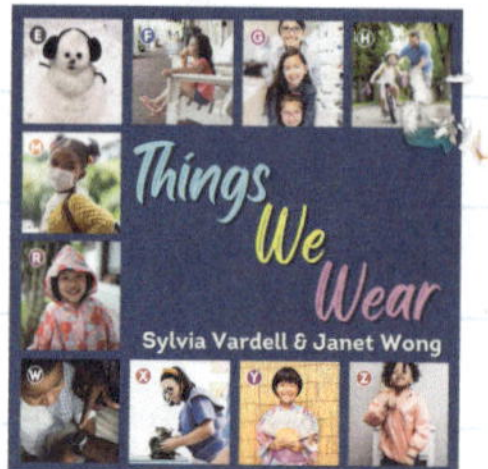

Things We Do - Things We Eat
Things We Feel - Things We Wear

CBC Hot Off the Press selections

IBBY Fundraiser Books

The ekphrastic poems in these books were written in response to full-color photographs of children in familiar settings: playing sports and games, cooking and eating, exploring nature, and spending time with friends and family. The books have an alphabet theme that can easily serve as a mentor text for a group project for older students, especially if students are given the task of taking photographs in their community.

Best Book for Educators + Administrators

GREAT MORNING! Poems for School Leaders to Read Aloud

A CBC Hot Off the Press selection

This book contains 75 poems for morning announcements or for the start of class. Principals, teachers, and student leaders will find poems on many useful topics from school safety to celebrating teamwork to honoring staff members such as the school nurse or custodian.

This book is dedicated to
all who bring CLARity
to this KOOKY world

Special thanks to
Renée M. LaTulippe for her ongoing help
in editing Pomelo Books publications –
and a heartfelt round of applause
to Willeena Booker, teacher extraordinaire,
and the many teachers and librarians
who share their love of poetry
with children.

A portion of the profits from this book
will be donated to charities
that bring joy to children in hospitals.

Pomelo Books
9440 Viewside Drive
Dallas, TX 75231
PomeloBooks.com
info@pomelobooks.com

ISBN 978-1-937057-86-2

Please visit us at PomeloBooks.com

Made in the USA
Columbia, SC
15 October 2024